NOV - - - 2023

Not That Fancy

Simple Lessons on Living, Loving, Eating, and Dusting Off Your Boots

REBA McENTIRE

HARPER
Celebrate

Published by Harper Celebrate, an imprint of HarperCollins Focus LLC.

Any internet addresses (websites, blogs, etc.) in this book are offered as a resource. They are not intended in any way to be or imply an endorsement by HarperCollins Focus LLC, nor does HarperCollins Focus LLC vouch for the content of these sites for the life of this book.

Photo page 258: Art Streiber/Kentucky Fried Chicken Corporation © Kentucky Fried Chicken Corporation. All rights reserved.
Photo page 261: John Russell/Country Music Association, Inc. © Country Music Association, Inc. All rights reserved.

Cover design by Sabryna Lugge
Interior design by Emily Ghattas
Lifestyle photography by Robby Klein Photography
Food photography by Kris D'Amico Photography

ISBN 978-1-4002-3827-9 (audiobook)
ISBN 978-1-4002-3826-2 (epub)
ISBN 978-1-4002-3825-5 (HC)
ISBN 978-1-4041-1967-3 (custom)
ISBN 978-1-4002-3513-1 (signature edition)
ISBN 978-1-4002-4850-6 (signature edition)

Printed in India

23 24 25 26 27   REP   10 9 8 7 6 5 4 3 2 1

Contents

Foreword

There are people you meet in life who actually shape you, shape your beliefs, even shape your dreams. Reba is one of those for me.

Growing up in Oklahoma, most of my friends ended up in the oil fields until the oil boom was over. Oklahoma was known for wheat, oil, and cattle, so if you didn't want to work in one of those jobs, the only way out of our small towns was sports or entertainment. Oklahoma has more than its share of famous athletes and entertainers, and I think Reba is one of our finest.

Reba was "everyone's girl" if you were from Oklahoma. Hell, Reba was your girl if you were from anywhere at all. With talent the likes of Patsy, Dolly, and Loretta, Reba also brought a business sense to entertainment. Not just "female" entertainment either. She brought a new business sense to entertainment period. She showed all of us that you can be sincere about your music and move the chess pieces at the same time.

For a kid from Oklahoma, Reba was the North Star pointing to my dream. If a kid from Stringtown, Oklahoma, could be a famous country singer, then there were no excuses why the rest of us couldn't follow in her footsteps. But with illumination, all things come to light—in order to have a career like Reba's, you're going to need some work ethic. Oh, sure, we can dream to be to country music what Reba is, but it's going to take a lot of work.

Reba took me under her wing and let me open one of her tours. It was a gift more precious than a four-year degree—learning from the University of Reba McEntire. I watched her lead her team, tirelessly cover every detail, see everything that could happen *before* it happened, steer her ship, and command the waters it was on. And the whole time, she was sincere, loving, and a servant to the music—the epitome of class.

As you'll see in this book, Reba is nothing fancy when it comes to being friends. She's not only the girl next door. She is also what the girl next door dreams of being. You can never forget she's a superstar, but it won't be Reba who reminds you. I don't know how she does it, but the great ones always do.

Garth Brooks

Introduction

When my mama died, I didn't know if I wanted to keep on singing. I just didn't have it in me. You see, my mama, Jac, has always been my reason for singing. Singing was her dream long before it was mine, and I've always done it for her. I've always been thankful to be blessed with an amazing career Mama could be proud of, but with her gone, I struggled to find my *why* anymore.

When Mama passed, I went back to the family home in Oklahoma to honor her life, help clean out Mama and Daddy's house, divide their belongings between us four kids, and spend some time visiting with my family. I thought I'd be there just a little while and then head right back to the packed tour schedule I had lined up.

But that was March 2020, and we had no clue what was about to change.

I've always been someone who likes to keep busy, lining up my next job before I've even finished the one I'm working on. But as I watched my usually full calendar of shows, meetings, and cross-country plane flights turn to a big old square of cancellations, I knew things were about to change. So I stayed there in Oklahoma for a little while with my siblings, Susie and Alice and Pake, reconnecting to the Oklahoma way of life.

I'm proud to be an Okie.

To me there's nothing better than sitting on the back porch looking out at the land that goes on for miles. A beautiful sunset, and then me, just sipping on a glass of iced tea (or whiskey and Sprite) with my friends and family. I don't know what heaven's going to look like, but I hope it feels like Oklahoma. Throw in some beans and cornbread, and I'm all set.

On the ranch, we make it a point to put God first, take care of our families, work hard, eat well, and always make time for a good, hearty laugh. We're not afraid of putting on our boots and getting a little dirty. Okies know that the secret to a good life is to keep things simple and be thankful for the things the good Lord's given you. Most of us probably

already know it in our bones, but when we get carried away with being busy, we forget that bigger isn't always better.

Not Mama. Mama never forgot, and I don't want to either.

Those few months of slowing down with the people I love in the place I know best helped me find my *why* again. My spark for singing is back stronger than ever. Susie said it would be. I'm still doing it for Mama.

Singing will always remind me of Mama, and I feel like she's right there with me when I'm singing.

But I'm also doing it for fun again. Everything I'm doing in my life from here on out—personal or professional, doesn't matter—I'm going to have fun. Enjoying what we've been given is one of the best ways I know to honor the Lord. I've been blessed beyond measure, and I want to make sure to never stop letting God know just how thankful I am for the life He's given me.

Relaxing in the sunshine during the pandemic at my home place, Eastern Oklahoma, 2020

Especially those not-that-fancy things, because as I've found, that's where my heart is.

So that's what I'm sharing in this book: the simple Oklahoma-style truths I keep coming back to and a bunch of good stories, photos, and recipes that go along with them. So if you're looking to slow down, get back to basics, and just have a heckuva lot of fun, then I think we're going to have a good time together in these pages. Come on in, kick off your boots (or leave them on, I don't care), and learn how to bring a little bit of my Western-inspired life into your own.

Let's have a good time, alright?

Love,

Reba McEntire

How to Use These Recipes

When I have friends over to my house, I like to make sure they feel taken care of and never leave with an empty stomach. Some of the dishes in this book are straight from my kitchen, and I'm also including some of my favorites from family and friends.

A lot of these recipes also come from my restaurant, Reba's Place, which I got to develop in partnership with the Choctaw Nation of Oklahoma. Chef Kurtess Mortensen is the genius behind our menu, which features some of my favorite Southwestern-style dishes and signature cocktails. We've adapted these recipes just for you, identified by our Reba's Place logo, to hold you over until you can take a trip to visit the restaurant in Atoka, Oklahoma, and experience it for yourself.

Some of these recipes are easier than others, so I've set up a rating system so you know exactly what you're getting into. I hope you'll add your own flair to these dishes and make them your own—as fancy or not that fancy as you like. Like I said, I'm all about keeping things simple, so you have my blessing to take shortcuts whenever you need. And if you mess up, there's always Sonic.

I wish there were a way for me to have one big potluck party with all of you reading this book, but until I can figure that out, I hope these recipes will be a blessing for you and your loved ones as you create lasting, loving memories together.

A Lot of Hope
and Hard Work

Some would say the McEntires are a very set-in-their-ways, stubborn, hardheaded bunch of people. But I think that hardheadedness is what got Daddy to where he was, Grandpap to where he was, and his father, Pap, to where he was. Some might say it wasn't all that far—but it was much further than where they started!

None of us McEntires came from money, but each generation's been a little more prosperous than the one before it. My daddy, Clark, was determined to make a better life for himself than the one he'd been handed. Like Grandpap before him, Daddy had the rodeo bug. He knew that rodeo couldn't pay all the bills, but it sure helped get him started.

Take for instance one time when Daddy won a roping competition. The prize was a new car and five hundred dollars cash. He gave it all to

My grandpap, John McEntire, competing at the Cheyenne Frontier Days, Cheyenne, Wyoming, 1934

Mama and sent her to swap it for eighty acres of land that Uncle Dale, Mama's brother, owned. That gave Daddy enough space to expand his ranch with more cattle. It was the start he needed. A few years later, in 1957, Daddy and Mama were able to buy a much bigger plot of land in Chockie, so he moved the family and all the cattle over there. Not exactly the land of milk and honey, but little by little, he was moving on up.

Land in Chockie was only $6.40 an acre, and there was good reason for that! A lot of neighbors called it "sorry land," and they warned Daddy not to buy it. It was rocky, hilly, and didn't grow much except briars and scrub brush, but he saw something no one else saw in that "sorry land." He turned a profit selling timber to the paper mill and rocks to the architects in Dallas. Then he struck gas.

That sorry land turned out to be worth more than anyone realized.

Daddy liked the rodeos, but he loved ranching. Rodeoing and selling timber, rocks, and natural gas all helped in the progression of our ranch. Daddy had to travel to compete in rodeos, but he wanted to be home on the ranch.

But ranch life is not an easy life. Maintaining the land and cattle takes time, and you can't skip a day just because you're worn out. Working the land was a whole family affair. The only times you wouldn't find us kids helping out was when we were in school. I thought that going to college would give me a break. Nope. I was wrong. Daddy had leased some land halfway between home and the Southeastern Oklahoma State University in Durant, Oklahoma. So every other day, after my classes, I loaded thirty fifty-pound sacks of feed into my pickup truck and fed the three hundred head of cattle.

Not quite the college experience everybody else had!

I didn't really know anything else though. I had started pitching in before I could even sit in a saddle. I don't remember exactly the first time I was on a horse, but it feels like I was born riding. Us kids spent a lot of time rounding up cattle. It was rough country, and often we'd have to ride through brush and briars taller than we were on the off chance we'd find even one lonely steer. There was always more work than hands to do it. We got cattle in the spring, straightened them up, and shipped them off to the feed lots in the fall.

Daddy's Three Rules to Live By

Daddy didn't have lots of rules for us kids because he trusted us to do the right thing. But the few rules he did have, well, you would never catch us breaking them while Daddy was around.

1. Don't play cards in the daytime.
2. Don't watch TV in the daytime.
3. Don't count your money.

The daytime was for work, and the evenings were for fun. And I do think that concept still holds true—you need time dedicated to work and time dedicated to relaxing. Daddy taught us to keep living right, in good times and bad.

✯ Helpful Henry ✯

Daddy had one roping steer whose horns started curling, which meant Daddy couldn't rope him anymore. We named him Henry, and he basically became a part of the ranch.

Henry was what we called the lead steer. All the other cattle would follow him without a thought. During the summer, the cattle roamed free in the hills, but when it came time to sell them in the fall, we'd have to round them all up. Of course, none of the cattle wanted to leave their territory, but Mama used Henry to her advantage. She'd drive down the road with feed in the back of the truck. Henry would follow right behind like a puppy dog trying to get to that feed, and like clockwork, the rest of the cattle would follow him. Us kids would ride behind on our horses, herding the cattle and chasing any stragglers who refused to go along nicely with the rest of the group.

And ol' Henry knew the drill. As Mama approached the corrals, Henry would turn around, jump the fences, and head back into the hills. But the rest of the cattle would stay with us, right where we needed them. Worked like a charm!

When Henry finally passed on due to cancer, we had his head mounted, which is the best way I could think of to honor my old friend and keep him close. He's with me still. I also have a kudu mounted and the skeleton of a deer I got from my land in Limestone Gap, Oklahoma. I love to walk through the living room and say, "Good mornin', boys!"

My older sister, Alice, my older brother, Pake, and me on one of Daddy's horses at our family ranch, Eastern Oklahoma, 1956

Daddy always had a plan to get the job done. Problem was, he wasn't the best at relaying his plan to the rest of us. He was usually looking the other direction or doing three things at once when he was giving us our instructions for the day. Most of the time, we only got a quarter of what he was trying to tell us. We always looked to Grandpap for an interpretation. I'm sure glad we had him to help us out!

The most important thing about helping out on the ranch was getting in line, doing your part, and following instructions. If our instructions were to sit at a gate until Daddy returned, under no circumstances were we going to abandon our posts. You sat at that gate until Daddy came back and told you that you could leave. It could be several hours, but that didn't matter. Hot or cold, rain or shine, you stayed glued to your saddle.

It was out there in those hills that I first learned that the work is in the waiting.

*Riding on the family ranch alongside
Daddy, Susie, Mama, Alice, and Pake
during the filming of my Reba: Starting Over
CBS TV special, Chockie, Oklahoma, 1995*

Fast-forward fifteen years, when I got into the music business. I knew less than nothing about how it all worked. I thought that once your record got on the radio, you got a tour bus and a big ol' check. You'd made it. You were a big star. *Wrong!*

I remember being so excited when I heard my debut single playing on our staticky, old radio for the very first time. Mama, Susie, and I were all sitting on the floor, crying with joy, thinking, *This is it.*

But then . . . not much happened. No fancy tour bus or big royalty check appeared. I felt pretty sure that God had called me to the dream of singing, but much like my daddy giving me instructions up in the hills, it felt like I had only gotten a fourth of what God said, and I knew I needed to wait for more information. So just like I learned as a kid, I stayed patient. And I kept working.

From hearing that first song on the radio, I spent the next seven years traveling around, playing everywhere I could, living on greasy burgers and corn dogs at truck stops and county fairs from Los Angeles to Boston—seven years of performing at fairs, rodeos, and honky-tonks, singing over bar brawls, tractor-pull competitions, and bull sales. Seven years of patience before I had a real hit, "Can't Even Get the Blues," in January 1983.

Even with that hit, the first time I headlined my own show, in 1984, only eight hundred people showed up, and I actually lost money. I had to write a check to get out of town because I didn't sell enough tickets. And I thought, *Welcome to the big time!* I sure did appreciate the few who did show up though!

Thank God for that McEntire determination.

When it came my turn to be a parent, I was determined to teach my son, Shelby, how important hard work is too, but I didn't need to worry. From an early age, Shelby was a very determined young man. He has a great work ethic. When it came time for him to start his own career, he put

How to Talk Like a Native Oklahoman

Oklahoma has a language all its own. Here's my translation guide for the next time you encounter an Oklahoman in the wild.

A **broom tail** means "an ugly, bad-tempered horse."

Chuck means "food."

Fair to middlin' means "pretty good."

Fit to be tied means "angry."

Jawing means "talking."

Madder than a wet hen means "super angry."

Off your feed means "not feeling well."

Piddlin' means "doing stuff other people might think is a waste of time" (mine and Susie's favorite pastime!).

Spinnin' yarns means "telling stories."

To strap on the feed bag means "to eat."

That dog won't hunt means "that's a bad idea."

his nose to the grindstone. When Shelby told me he wanted to be a race car driver, I wanted to help but had no clue where to start. If there had been a *Racing for Dummies* book, I would have bought ten. I asked anyone I could think of for information, but no one I knew had much advice to give. Scott Borchetta, head of Big Machine Records and a former race car driver himself, told me to buy him a go-kart. But Shelby already had a go-kart!

So, we bought Shelby a membership to the Skip Barber Racing School. It's a school that teaches kids the racing business, and it allowed him to race in as many races as possible. You have to pay your dues in racing, just like you do in the rodeo and music businesses. Shelby raced in the Southern and the Western series. He drove eight to nine races a day for three days every weekend. I gave him my airline miles and hotel points

Hanging with Shelby at the race car track

from years of touring, and he flew on Southwest and stayed in the cheapest motels to make the most of it. Funny part was, he was too young to rent a car, so he had to get a taxi or bum a ride to the track.

Shelby could have followed his daddy's, Narvel Blackstock's, footsteps into music management, but he chose to chart his own course. He's now into real estate and developing property. You don't think your kids listen to half of what you tell them, but Shelby did. I'm so proud of him. He's kind and confident and is building a life that he's proud of and that makes him happy. And he still wants me to be a big part of that. I am so grateful.

Most of what you hope for in this life takes time and some old-fashioned stick-to-itiveness. None of us in the McEntire family were overnight successes. From generation to generation, we just keep learning, dreaming, and working hard. One thing I'm sure of: good things won't come if you give up and go home.

Cowgirl Baked Beans

DIFFICULTY

8 slices bacon, cut in half crosswise

1 yellow onion, finely chopped

6 (15-ounce) cans pork and beans

½ cup Reba's Place Tangy Barbecue Sauce (p. 217)

⅓ cup brown sugar, packed

2 tablespoons ketchup

1 tablespoon steak sauce

2 teaspoons yellow mustard

1 teaspoon Worcestershire sauce

Kosher salt, to taste

Freshly ground black pepper, to taste

> These quantities are perfect for a potluck. For a smaller crowd, halve the ingredients and bake in a 2-quart dish.

Baked beans were a staple in our house growing up. This is my little-bit-fancy version, and I think these beans go well with just about anything.

1. Preheat the oven to 325°F. Spray a 4-quart baking dish with nonstick cooking spray.

2. Set an extra-large skillet over medium-high heat and add the bacon. Fry until just browned but not fully cooked and crispy.

3. Transfer the bacon from the skillet to a plate. Add the onions to the bacon drippings in the skillet. Sauté until softened and lightly browned, about 5 to 6 minutes.

4. Pour the pork and beans into a large mixing bowl. Add the onions, Reba's Place Tangy Barbecue Sauce, brown sugar, ketchup, steak sauce, mustard, and Worcestershire. Season with salt and pepper, to taste. Mix until the ingredients are thoroughly combined.

5. Pour the beans into the baking dish and lay the bacon slices on top. Transfer to the middle rack of the oven.

6. Bake for 1 hour, or until the beans are bubbling at the edges. Remove the dish from the oven. Allow to rest for 15 to 20 minutes, or until slightly thickened, before serving.

Lucchese's Pork Tenderloin

DIFFICULTY 🥄 🥄 🥄

2 pounds pork tenderloin (1 large)

Kosher salt, to taste

Freshly ground black pepper, to taste

1¹/₂ tablespoons olive oil, divided

1 stalk celery, roughly chopped

¹/₂ small yellow onion, roughly chopped

1 carrot, peeled and roughly chopped

2 cups beef or chicken broth

¹/₃ cup red wine

1 tablespoon water

1 teaspoon cornstarch

This melt-in-your-mouth pork tenderloin is courtesy of my niece Lucchese, Susie's daughter. It's easy to make, but no one would ever guess because it looks and tastes so fancy!

1. Preheat the oven to 350°F.

2. Season the pork tenderloin liberally with salt and pepper. Set an extra-large cast-iron skillet over medium-high heat and add 1 tablespoon of olive oil.

3. Sear the pork until deeply golden, turning it to brown all sides, about 5 to 6 minutes. Remove the skillet from the heat.

4. Arrange the celery, onion, and carrots around the pork. Drizzle with the remaining ¹/₂ tablespoon of olive oil and sprinkle with salt and pepper. Transfer the skillet to the middle rack of the oven.

5. Roast for 30 to 35 minutes, or until the pork reaches an internal temperature of 140°F. Remove the skillet from the oven.

6. Carefully lift the pork from the skillet and transfer it to a cutting board. Cover it loosely with foil to keep warm.

7. Return the skillet to the stove over medium-high heat. Sauté the vegetables for 2 to 3 minutes, then pour the broth and red wine into the skillet. Stir, scraping up any browned bits until the liquid simmers.

8. In a small bowl, whisk together the water and cornstarch. Pour the mixture into the skillet and stir it into the simmering broth.

9. Continue simmering until the sauce starts to bubble and thicken, about 2 minutes. Remove the skillet from the heat. Lift the vegetables from the sauce with a fork and discard.

10. Slice the pork tenderloin ¾-inch thick on a diagonal and transfer to a serving platter. Drizzle with the sauce and serve immediately with your favorite vegetable side.

2

Nature Is My Church

Nature is the church I go to when I want to feel closer to God. That's where my angels find me. I call them *angels*, but I don't know if they're actual angels or the Holy Spirit. What I do know is that I never feel alone when I'm standing under an open sky. Maybe it stems from those summer afternoons when I was a little girl, listening to our Grandma Smith tell us Bible stories while we fished at her pond. Or maybe it's just because of all the time I've spent riding horses.

I first learned about Jesus and His love for us from Grandma, the one I was named after: Reba Estelle Smith, Mama's mama. I remember us kids going to the one-room church house there in Chockie, Oklahoma, where Grandpa and Grandma Smith were regulars. I later accepted Jesus as my personal Savior and was baptized at the Kiowa Baptist Church when I was twelve years old. That was the first time, but it wasn't the last.

Sing It Out

God and music have always gone hand in hand for me. I love to sing for the Lord. Even if you can't carry a tune in a bucket, go ahead and sing anyway. God loves a joyful noise. Here are my favorites to get you started.

---

* **"Jesus Loves Me."** This is one of the first gospel songs I ever learned from Grandma Smith. I also sang this as a kid in the Edwards Hotel lobby in Cheyenne, Wyoming, in the late fifties and earned a nickel for it. The first time I ever got paid for singing!

* **"Amazing Grace/My Chains Are Gone."** I sang the updated version of this classic on the *My Chains Are Gone* album. Singing it gives me chills every time.

* **"Because He Lives."** I love our rendition of this Bill Gaither classic on the *My Chains Are Gone* album. We did it as a shuffle $^4/_4$ Western swing song.

* **"I'd Rather Have Jesus."** This one speaks to my heart so deeply. The first time I heard it was on Loretta Lynn's album. Talk about a woman who loved the Lord.

* **"Softly and Tenderly."** I have the best memories of singing this with Kelly Clarkson and Trisha Yearwood.

* **"How Great Thou Art."** This old hymn was one of Grandma Smith's favorites, and I can't sing it without getting emotional.

* **"Back to God."** I've loved this song ever since I heard it on Randy Houser's album, and it was such a joy to sing it with my friend Lauren Daigle.

* **"When the Roll Is Called Up Yonder."** This song always takes me back to being in that little one-room Chockie church as a kid.

* **"I'll Fly Away."** This has been a favorite since childhood. Alice, Susie, Mama, and I got to sing it at the Ryman Auditorium in 2017. I'm so glad we have those moments on tape. I love singing with my family. I sure wish Pake could have been there too!

* **"The Lord's Prayer."** I got to sing this song at former president George H. W. Bush's funeral. It was the honor of a lifetime.

I don't think you accept Jesus and that's that. It's a choice you have to keep making throughout your life, a choice to keep following Him above all.

The second time I accepted Jesus into my heart was in 1978. I saw my friend Willard Moody at the Copenhagen/Skoal roping event in Fort Worth, Texas. We prayed together in the barn. I rededicated my life to Jesus right then and there, in a dusty horse stall. As soon as we said "Amen," I felt so much better.

Left: Singing at president George H. W. Bush's funeral, Houston, Texas, 2018

Right: Susie, Mama, Alice, and me singing "I'll Fly Away" the first time I headlined the Ryman Auditorium, Nashville, Tennessee, 2017

I'm grateful that all six of my immediate family members have been saved. It's a wonderful thing to know that we'll all get to be together again someday in heaven. Alice, Susie, and I, we've always had faith since we were young girls, and Pake found his walk with Jesus a little later in life. So glad! But I know everybody has to find their faith in their own time.

Daddy got saved in 1980. He had heard and seen enough about Jesus that he just believed. When he was ready, he was proud to go down the aisle in front of the church and be baptized. I think it took a load off his mind. He was very logical about most things in life, and his faith wasn't any different.

His reasoning was that if Jesus gave us the gift of salvation, why wouldn't we accept that free gift? I think that's a really good way to look at it.

I remember one Sunday long before Daddy was saved, while Herman Edge was preaching, Daddy raised his hand.

"Clark," Preacher Edge said, "we can take questions after we get through here."

"Well, I might not remember my question by then," Daddy replied.

We all got a chuckle out of that.

Mama was saved in 2015, at the young age of eighty-nine, when she decided she was finally ready to invite God in. According to my cousin Trisha Ann and my oldest sister, Alice, Mama went to church that Sunday morning in April, and when it was time for the altar call (that's where people walk the aisle to go ask to be saved), Mama walked up to the front and said, "Preacher, I'm turning myself in. I'm tired of doing this all by myself." *Boy, does that hit home!*

When Mama took the journey to go to heaven in March 2020, I had a peace that she was up there visiting with Daddy and all of her friends and family who had gone on before her. It puts my heart at ease knowing I will see them together again one day.

I love to talk to God, and I've never been shy about asking Him for a helping hand. Doesn't matter if a problem is big or small, I talk to God about it. But Daddy saw it a different way. Back when I first started singing, Mama let me wear one of Daddy's championship belt buckles. You can see it on the cover of my album *Whoever's in New England*. At one point, when I came home from touring, I realized I'd misplaced it. Daddy overheard me tell Mama that I'd been praying I would find that lost belt buckle.

"Reba," Daddy said, "don't bother God with silly stuff like that. He's got more important things to deal with."

Talkin' to God

There are many ways to pray to the Lord. Here are a few you can try if you're feeling stuck about how to talk to Him.

* **Sing a song.** The Bible talks about music an awful lot, and singing has always been part of the way we worship God. I love the praise-and-worship part of church and feel so close to Him when I'm singing.

* **Ask the Holy Spirit to take over.** When you don't have the words, the Holy Spirit does.

* **Recite the Lord's Prayer.** Let that be your starting point.

* **Get out into nature.** Just be still. Listen for God instead of doing all the talking.

* **Read your Bible.** Get into God's Word and see what He tells you.

* **Ask someone else to pray with you.** We all know a few prayer warriors we can ask to help us out if we need it.

On the set of the "Back to God" video shoot at the historic Tulip Street United Methodist Church, Nashville, Tennessee, 2017

Running barrels at the family ranch during the Reba: Starting Over CBS TV special, Chockie, Oklahoma, 1995

Hugging the first horse I ever owned, Old Sonny, when I was just twenty-one years old, Eastern Oklahoma, 1976

Life on Horseback

As I said earlier, I feel God the most in nature, and many of my younger days in nature were spent on horseback. I was a grown woman before I had a horse of my own, so until then I rode Pake's and Daddy's roping horses. Here are some of the best horses I've ever had the privilege to ride.

- ★ **Ole Pelican.** He was the first barrel-racing horse I rode in my first rodeo at the age of eleven. I called him Ole Paint.

- ★ **Old Bay.** He was one of Daddy's steer-roping horses. Pake roped on him sometimes too, which was actually pretty impressive, because Daddy roped right-handed and Pake roped left-handed. Old Bay was smart enough to know the difference!

- ★ **Old Silky.** Silky was Pake's calf-ropin' horse. He wasn't doing too well so Pake asked me to keep Old Silky in shape by running barrels on him. It was on Old Silky that I filled my GRA permit in Lubbock, Texas, and San Angelo, Texas, for the Girls Rodeo Association—now the Women's Professional Rodeo Association—to become a bona fide cowgirl.

- ★ **Old Sonny.** This was the first horse I ever owned. I was married and twenty-one years old when I bought him.

- ★ **Yeller.** Yeller was my horse after Sonny. I didn't get to ride him as often as I would have liked because I was always on the road back then.

- ★ **Legs.** Legs was the sweetest, gentlest sorrel horse. He wasn't flighty like a bulldog horse or barrel-racing horse, and I loved riding him.

- ★ **Gator.** Nowadays, Gator is my horse. He's easy to ride, has the best personality, and keeps us all laughing.

That really shocked me because I asked God about everything!

Later on, when I came home from touring, I called Mama. She told me that my nephew, Vince, and our neighbor's son had found the belt buckle in the dried-up creek bed! It might seem like a small answer to prayer, but it was a huge reminder for me that prayer works. There is nothing too big or too small to pray to God about. He can do the impossible. You just have to ask.

The main thing I try to stay consistent with in my life is my relationship with the Lord. He's always been there for me. My faith has gotten me through the loneliest of times. He's that rock, that fortress you lean on when things go wrong.

The best way for me to be still in my spirit is to go out for a long walk. I love being outside and looking at God's creation. Watching the clouds go by and listening to the birds sing always fills me with peace. I felt the same way when I was a girl riding through the hills on our ranch. There's just something about being alone in nature that helps me listen in a way I can't in the middle of the hustle and bustle of my usual life.

Riding on the family ranch, Chockie, Oklahoma, 1995

One day back in 2014, when I was out walking, I said, "Okay, Lord. What do You want me to do?" and He said, "Pray for peace." So I did. A few days later I was out walking again, and I asked again, "Lord, what do You want me to do?" and again He said, "Pray for peace."

"Well, I've been doing that."

"Sing it," He said.

So I started singing, "Pray for peace. Pray for peace."

A while after that, I asked God what He wanted me to do with that song, and He said, "Record it."

So we did. We recorded it and made a music video that included people from all over the world praying for peace. I was so moved to see the Lord at work in the lives of so many different people in so many different places. I don't write a lot of songs, but when the Lord gives you such clear direction, you listen.

When I'm going through something tough, most of the time God just wants me to be still and listen to the instructions He's giving. It's about His time, not my time. His will, His way. Not mine.

Another time when I was out walking, trying to process through my divorce, I heard God say, "When something like this happens, just say, 'Oh well.'" So that's what I do. Or sometimes I tell Him, "Okay, Big Boy. I can't handle this. This is way over my pay grade." And every time, He shows up and takes care of me.

When tough times come, we have to recognize that this life is not our own. Sometimes there is nothing we can do but get out of the way and let God take control. I have full faith that God is in control and that He is bringing better things into my life, even if I can't see them yet.

God is always there when you need Him. You might find Him in church, or you may be like me and feel closer to Him out in His creation. Get out in nature and let all the things God has made show you the way. Faith is never far away, and at least for me, the best evidence that God is always with us is right outside. I hope these words will help you to be still and listen for Him. And I hope you'll find in Him what I always have—love, strength, peace, and wisdom.

Bring the Outside In

As someone who loves the outdoors, I make sure I bring natural elements indoors wherever I can. Here's my guide to bringing the outside in.

* **Make it personal.** I like to combine photos and souvenirs from my travels through Africa mixed with Western-inspired elements like rich leathers and dark woods. My style is a little tough, a little bold, and a little edgy. I call it "tough sexy." I take photos of landscapes and animals, and I get so much joy out of seeing my own photos hanging on my walls.

* **Hone in on a region that inspires you.** I love Pendleton wool blankets. They remind me of the time many years ago when Daddy came home from the Pendleton Round-Up rodeo with one. I still have it in my home today. Mounted steer heads and antlers bring me back to that feeling I had growing up on the ranch. And warmth from plants and natural stone tiles helps tie everything together. Find a place you feel connected to and blend that in your décor.

* **Incorporate plants.** Easy-to-care-for succulents and houseplants in pretty pots will bring life to any room. Fake plants can work just as well. I also love to have fresh-cut red roses around the house. Sometimes I cut a few branches off a tree in the yard, but other times I just grab some flowers from the grocery store. I like to get a few different groupings of mixed flowers and arrange them in several smaller bouquets to place throughout our home.

* **Draw the eyes outdoors.** Got a great window view? You'll always find my curtains wide open so I can enjoy the view of the Tennessee hills. I make sure to plant flowering shrubs or trees with beautiful fall colors where I'll be able to see and enjoy them during every season. We also set up bird feeders around the yard, and we like to sit and name all the different kinds of birds who come to visit us.

Scenes around my home, Nashville, Tennessee

Porch Day Lemonade

DIFFICULTY

Not much beats sitting on the porch on a warm summer day, taking in the beauty of the outdoors, with an ice-cold glass of lemonade in hand.

1 cup water, plus more to fill the pitcher

1 cup sugar

Juice from 6 to 8 lemons

Fresh basil leaves for garnish (optional)

1. Place the water and sugar in a medium saucepan and set over medium-high heat. Bring to a low simmer.

2. Heat for about 5 minutes, stirring occasionally, until the sugar is dissolved. Remove the saucepan from the heat.

3. Pour the liquid into a 2-quart pitcher and allow to cool.

4. In the meantime, juice the lemons. Use 6 for a sweeter lemonade, or 8 if you like your lemonade tart.

5. Pour the lemon juice into the pitcher and stir to combine. Fill the remainder of the pitcher with cold water, and stir once more.

6. To serve, pour the lemonade into tall glasses of ice. For something a little different, garnish with fresh basil leaves.

Like It Fancy?

For an especially hot day, I recommend switching things up to create frozen lemonade. Replace half of the water with ice and pour into a blender. Blend on high until you have a nice slushy texture. Serve in chilled glasses for ultimate refreshment.

Shishito Peppers and Okra with Tequila Lime Vinaigrette

MAKES 4 SERVINGS
PREP TIME: 20 MINUTES
COOK TIME: 10 MINUTES

DIFFICULTY

TEQUILA LIME VINAIGRETTE

½ cup fresh lime juice (4 to 6 limes)

2 tablespoons tequila

2 tablespoons agave syrup

1 tablespoon rice wine vinegar

1 teaspoon Dijon mustard

1 clove garlic, minced

2 tablespoons fresh cilantro leaves, finely chopped

½ teaspoon kosher salt, more to taste

½ cup canola oil

PEPPERS AND OKRA

3 cups shishito peppers, rough stems removed (about 12 ounces)

1½ cups fresh okra, sliced in half lengthwise (about 6 ounces)

2 tablespoons olive oil, divided

Kosher salt, to taste

Freshly ground black pepper, to taste

¼ cup Reba's Place Tequila Lime Vinaigrette

1 wedge each lime and orange, for garnish

It's always good to have a little green on the plate! But what can I say, I prefer my greens fried!

TEQUILA LIME VINAIGRETTE

MAKES 1¼ CUPS

1. Place the lime juice, tequila, syrup, vinegar, mustard, garlic, cilantro, salt, and oil into a large shaker cup or dressing bottle. Secure the lid and shake vigorously until the dressing is emulsified. Refrigerate until ready to use.

PEPPERS AND OKRA

1. Preheat the oven to 450°F. Line a baking sheet with parchment paper.

2. Place the shishitos and okra in a colander and rinse under cool water. Drain on a few sheets of paper towels.

3. Place the okra in a mixing bowl and drizzle with 1 tablespoon of olive oil. Sprinkle liberally with salt and toss to coat. Spread the okra in a single layer on the baking sheet and transfer to the middle rack of the oven.

4. Bake for 10 to 12 minutes, flipping halfway through, until the okra is tender and lightly browned. Remove the baking sheet from the oven and transfer the okra back to the mixing bowl.

5. While the okra roasts, set a cast-iron skillet over high heat and add the remaining 1 tablespoon of olive oil. Once the oil is smoking, add the shishito peppers in single layer. Sprinkle liberally with salt.

6. Cover the skillet with a lid and allow the shishitos to blister for 15 to 25 seconds. Stir the peppers, cover, and cook for 15 to 25 seconds more, or until the peppers are well-charred. Remove the skillet from the heat.

7. Add the shishitos to the bowl of okra. Drizzle with vinaigrette and additional salt and pepper, to taste. Toss until the vegetables are evenly coated.

8. Transfer the shishitos and okra to a serving dish and garnish with a lime and orange wedge. Serve immediately.

Carrot Cake

MAKES 12 TO 16 SERVINGS
PREP TIME: 35 MINUTES
COOK TIME: 35 MINUTES
INACTIVE TIME: 3 HOURS

DIFFICULTY

This cake must be healthy with all the carrots in it, right? Keep any leftover carrots to treat your horses.

CAKE

1 cup brown sugar, packed

3/4 cup white sugar

3/4 cup canola or vegetable oil

4 eggs

2 teaspoons vanilla extract

2 1/4 cups all-purpose flour

2 teaspoons baking powder

1 teaspoon baking soda

2 teaspoons cinnamon

1/2 teaspoon nutmeg

1/2 teaspoon salt

3 cups finely grated carrots (5 to 6 medium carrots)

1 cup chopped pecans (optional)

FROSTING

2 (8-ounce) bars cream cheese, room temperature

2 sticks (1 cup) salted butter, room temperature

4 1/2 cups powdered sugar

2 teaspoons vanilla extract

CAKE

1. Preheat the oven to 350°F. Spray two 8- or 9-inch round cake pans with nonstick cooking spray.

2. Place the sugars, oil, eggs, and vanilla in a large bowl and whisk vigorously to combine.

3. Add the flour, baking powder, baking soda, cinnamon, nutmeg, and salt to the bowl. Mix until it forms a smooth batter. Fold in the carrots and pecans (if using).

4. Divide the batter evenly between the baking pans. Transfer to the middle rack of the oven.

5. Bake for 33 to 37 minutes, or until a toothpick inserted in the center of the cake comes out clean. Remove the pans from the oven. Allow the cakes to rest in the pans for 10 minutes, then invert them onto a wire rack to cool completely before frosting.

FROSTING

1. Place the cream cheese and butter in a large mixing bowl. Beat with a hand mixer on medium speed until smooth, about 3 minutes. Add the powdered sugar and vanilla. Beat on low speed until most of the sugar is absorbed into the cream cheese mixture, then increase the speed to medium-high and continue beating until the frosting is creamy, about 2 minutes.

2. To assemble: With a sharp knife, carefully slice the cooled cake layers in half crosswise, creating 4 layers. Place one layer on a serving platter and spread a $\frac{1}{2}$-inch thick layer of frosting on top. Repeat with the remaining three cake layers. Frost the sides of the cake with the remaining frosting, then use the back of a spoon to create rustic swoops over the top and sides of the cake. Refrigerate for at least 1 hour before slicing and serving.

3

Wear What You Want (And Put Some Fringe on It)

I've always more or less known who I am and what I like. That hasn't really changed over the years, especially when it comes to my style. Growing up, we didn't have a lot. Mama wasn't much into fashion, and she wasn't going to spend money on clothes when we had more important things to buy. So I got used to making do with what I had.

We had cousins in Texas who would send us boxes of their hand-me-downs when they got tired of or outgrew them—clothes like nothing we'd ever seen. We got clothes like red velvet bell-bottom Western pants and fringed shirts with rhinestones all over them. You know, high fashion for the late 1960s.

One night when I was heading out to a football game, I put together what I thought was just the most stylish outfit—black stirrup pants, a white ruffled shirt, and black patent-leather pointed-toe flats two sizes too big. I strutted past the bleachers with the confidence of a supermodel, thinking, *Dang, I look good*, even though I was gripping those shoes with all my might just to keep them on my feet. I was scrunching my toes, hanging on by my toenails. But I owned the look, and that's what made it work, at least in my mind.

Other than those patent-leather flats, I was never really too concerned about how I looked, but it's always mattered to me that I felt comfortable. When the weather got warm enough in the spring to start riding, the first thing I would do after school was throw on my favorite big old sweatshirt with the sleeves cut off. I'd wear it to go exercise the horses, and the next day, I'd turn that sweatshirt around and wear it again. The next day, I'd turn it inside out and wear it. And then the fourth day, I'd turn it around and wear it again. All that before washing it. That poor sweatshirt started out white, but by the end of each week it was pretty dirty. But I was comfortable.

Belting out the national anthem at the National Finals Rodeo, Oklahoma City, Oklahoma

Later on, when I started getting more singing jobs, Mama asked our school bus driver's wife, Millie Wilson, if she would make me an outfit. Mama got the material from New York, and Millie made me an outfit that I absolutely loved. It was a blue satin shirt with a vest made of eyelash material to wear onstage. I can't really tell you if it was fashionable or not because I've never really cared about trends. Heck, back then I didn't even know what a trend was! But I felt like a star when I wore it.

Clothes Every Cowgirl Should Own

Whether you're a real, bona fide ropin' cowgirl or you just want to dress like one, here are the essentials you should have in your closet.

A great pair of jeans that fits well and makes you feel like a million bucks

Worn jeans. I like a thicker denim that will hold up when you're chewin' gravel and muckin' out stalls.

A leather vest, preferably with some fringe

Button-down denim shirts and flannel shirts, layered over a good tank top

A suede leather jacket. Again, I love some fringe!

A dress you can twirl in for going out dancing at the local honky-tonk

Silver and turquoise Western-style jewelry that can be worn from day to night

A sturdy leather belt and (hopefully) a trophy belt buckle

Once my career started taking off, I worked with stylists because I knew they knew a lot more than I did about fashion. Unfortunately, it took a few years before comfort won out. I had to wear high heels and clothes that weren't as comfortable as I would have liked. Eventually, I found what looked good *and* felt good. When it comes down to it, you have to wear what feels right to you. When I'm comfortable, I can be me!

In 2005, while I was out in L.A. working on the television show *Reba*, I was approached by Dillard's about starting my own fashion line. No one had *ever* called me fashionable before. Heck, the one time I went to Fashion Week in New York City, someone asked me who my favorite designer was and I said, "Levi's." Anyway, Dillard's assured me I wouldn't have to design anything myself. They would put together some ideas, and all I had to do was choose which ones I liked. Sounds easy, right?

It was not easy. After their first presentation, I politely told them that I wouldn't wear anything they had shown me. It just wasn't me. I spent a lot of time after that going through magazines and pulling pictures of

Josephine DiMarco and me collaborating on my Dillard's clothing line

things that I would actually wear. I sent my preferences directly to the designer with notes and she ran with them.

That designer is Josephine DiMarco , and she's still the designer for my clothing line today. It's been a great partnership! When we started out together, I would help out with the process of choosing fabrics, trim, buttons, and zippers. It took so long. After a while, she figured out what I like, and now she presents the clothes to me when they come in as samples. I'm so glad that women everywhere can feel comfortable and confident in my clothes.

Singing the national anthem at the National Finals Rodeo, Oklahoma City, Oklahoma

In 2017 I also got the chance to work with Justin Boots. Now, Justin Boots has been part of my story since the beginning. In December 1974, I sang the national anthem at the National Finals Rodeo in Oklahoma City. It was at this performance where Red Steagall— the man who was responsible for getting me to Nashville—heard me sing for the very first time. He said, "That little redheaded girl started singing, and it just blew me away."

A Boot for Every Mood

I think every woman should own three types of boots:

* **One casual pair** of everyday boots that are truly day-to-night. You can wear them around town, while traveling, or for a fun Saturday night out.

* **One rugged square-toe pair** for riding or spending time on the ranch.

* **One gorgeous go-to pair** built for attention, with stunning stitching and signature details. Fancy boots are always the finishing touch to my look when I go onstage. Or if you want to wear them to the grocery store, that's fine with me!

After the rodeo performance, Red invited Mama, Pake, Susie, and me up to the Justin Boots Suite at the Hilton where cowboys gathered for a guitar pull and to visit. At some point in the evening, Everett Shaw, a world-champion cowboy, asked me to sing Dolly Parton's hit song "Joshua." I sang it a cappella, and the next month, Red invited Mama and me to Nashville so I could record a demo.

So decades later, when I had the opportunity to partner with Justin Boots, it just felt right. While I may not have always known my way around fashion, I definitely know my way around a good pair of boots.

You can't be a cowgirl without them! I've worn my fair share of different types of boots over the years: from plain ones for working on the ranch, to riding boots for rodeoing, to fancy Western pairs with fringe and rhinestones for performing. My partnership with Justin Boots was so much fun that I suggested we do a line of comfy and cool sneakers for cowgirls to change into after they were done riding for the day. I love wearing them, and I'm so glad we have them in our collection!

Style is about more than just the clothes and shoes you wear. It's also about how you carry yourself. Hair and makeup are a big part of that. I'll never forget the time back in 1996 when I cut off my hair. My hair was so big

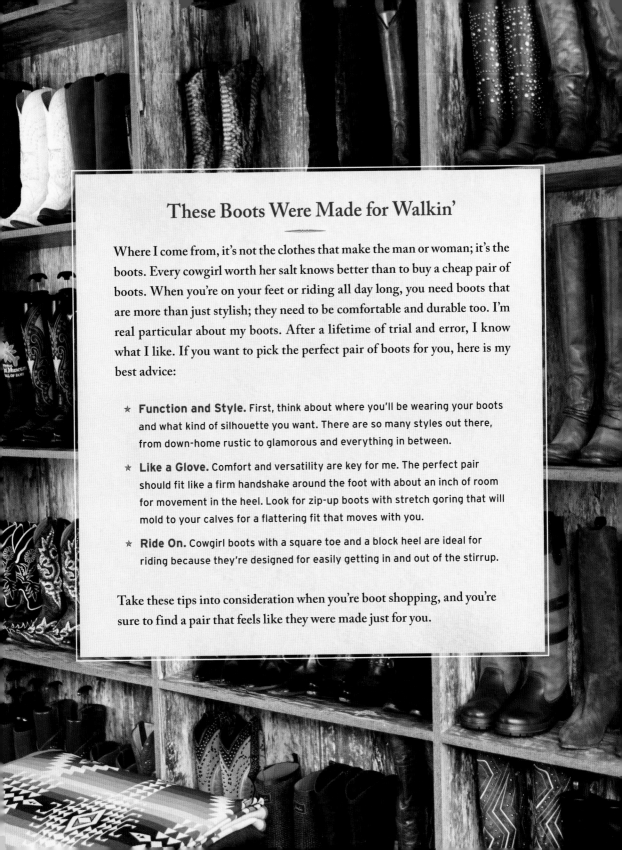

These Boots Were Made for Walkin'

Where I come from, it's not the clothes that make the man or woman; it's the boots. Every cowgirl worth her salt knows better than to buy a cheap pair of boots. When you're on your feet or riding all day long, you need boots that are more than just stylish; they need to be comfortable and durable too. I'm real particular about my boots. After a lifetime of trial and error, I know what I like. If you want to pick the perfect pair of boots for you, here is my best advice:

★ **Function and Style.** First, think about where you'll be wearing your boots and what kind of silhouette you want. There are so many styles out there, from down-home rustic to glamorous and everything in between.

★ **Like a Glove.** Comfort and versatility are key for me. The perfect pair should fit like a firm handshake around the foot with about an inch of room for movement in the heel. Look for zip-up boots with stretch goring that will mold to your calves for a flattering fit that moves with you.

★ **Ride On.** Cowgirl boots with a square toe and a block heel are ideal for riding because they're designed for easily getting in and out of the stirrup.

Take these tips into consideration when you're boot shopping, and you're sure to find a pair that feels like they were made just for you.

Jack It Up to Jesus

My friend Dolly Parton is famous for saying, "The higher the hair, the closer to God."
So if you want to get one of my signature looks, get your comb ready for some teasing.

80s

90s

00s

Now

80s: *It's not the eighties without a perm.*
1: Apply a generous amount of mousse to towel-dried hair. 2: Blow-dry and scrunch hair. 3: Select and apply heavy-duty hair spray.

90s: *Plug in your hot rollers.*
1: Follow steps 1 and 2 of my style from the 1980s. 2: Add hot rollers to dry scrunched hair. 3: Pick out curls and tease to desired height and fullness. 4: Spray with mega-hold hair spray. I like Aveda Witch Hazel.

00s: *Break out that flat iron.*
1: Blow-dry hair using a round brush to smooth and straighten. 2: Flat-iron random sections for a flippy style. 3: Finish with pomade for a wild and less structured look.

Now: *Less is more.*
1: Blow out hair with a medium round brush, and add styling cream for smoothness. 2: Curl hair with a 1.5-inch barrel curling iron for a soft, sophisticated style. 3: Spray with a light hair spray for desired height and fullness.

back in those days that my fans could recognize me just from my silhouette. But I didn't just wake up like that. It took hot rollers, more hot rollers, teasing, and enough hair spray to choke a horse.

I had wanted to cut it for a long time. But that big hair had been my signature look for more than a decade, so the thought of changing it made my team nervous.

An entertainer cutting her hair today might not exactly be breaking news, but the nineties was a very different time. Once you found something that worked, you stuck with it, come hell or high water. Long hair was part of the expected look for a country singer back then, but I was just tired of it. It needed to go.

When my team realized I'd made up my mind, they made the big cut part of the marketing plan for my upcoming album, *What If It's You*. I had actually cut my hair off in June, but the album didn't release until November, so I had to wear a wig until we were ready to reveal the new look. I finally debuted my short hair at the Country Music Association (CMA) Awards show, and it felt so good!

Top: Locks of my curls lying on the beach after my big haircut, 1996

Bottom: The album cover of What If It's You, debuting my new short hair, 1996

My new look kept reporters busy for several weeks, and in the end, *What If It's You* outsold my previous few albums and went double platinum. So I guess you could say it worked. (Now the songs were great too!) A new style may seem like a small thing, but it helped me feel more like myself, and I think my fans liked that. It just goes to show—trust your gut and do what's right for you. Everyone else will catch up.

That's the type of confidence we should all be shooting for every single day!

Chicken Tenders

MAKES 6 SERVINGS
PREP TIME: 20 MINUTES
COOK TIME: 20 MINUTES
INACTIVE TIME: 1 HOUR OR MORE

DIFFICULTY

4 (6-ounce) boneless, skinless chicken breasts

1½ cups bread-and-butter pickle juice

1 quart peanut oil (or vegetable oil), for frying

2 cups all-purpose flour

1 cup masa harina (also called "corn masa" or "corn flour")

1 cup finely ground low-sodium saltines (about 40 crackers)

1½ teaspoons seasoned salt (like Lawry's), or more, to taste

1 teaspoon chili powder

1 teaspoon freshly ground black pepper

1 teaspoon granulated garlic

1 teaspoon granulated onion

4 egg whites

1 tablespoon water

1 small handful fresh parsley, finely chopped, for garnish (optional)

½ cup Reba's Place Homemade Ranch Dressing, for serving (p. 49)

½ cup Reba's Place Cherry Coke Barbecue Sauce, for serving (p. 176)

Chicken tenders are my comfort food of choice when I'm performing out on the road, and I've been known to eat them immediately after getting offstage. Turns out they pair well with sweatshirts or sequins—up to you!

1. Slice each chicken breast into three long strips. Pound them lightly with a meat mallet to even out the thickness. Place the strips in a bowl with the pickle juice and let soak for at least 1 hour, preferably overnight.

2. When ready to fry the chicken, attach a thermometer to the side of a large Dutch oven and add the peanut oil. Heat the oil to 350°F and maintain the temperature within a range of 25°F. Line a baking sheet with parchment paper. Set a cooling rack on top of a second baking sheet and place it next to the Dutch oven.

3. While the oil heats, place the flour, masa harina, saltines, seasoned salt, chili powder, pepper, garlic, and onion in a large bowl and whisk to combine. In a separate bowl, whisk together the egg whites and water until lightly frothy.

4. Drain the pickle juice from the chicken. Transfer the strips to the bowl of egg whites, and stir to coat. Dip the strips one at a time into the flour mixture, turning to coat evenly, and arrange them on the baking sheet.

5. Fry the chicken strips in batches of 4 until golden brown, about 4 to 5 minutes. Remove the strips from the oil with a slotted spoon and transfer to the cooling rack. Repeat with the remaining chicken.

6. Garnish the chicken tenders with fresh parsley and serve with Reba's Place Homemade Ranch Dressing and Reba's Place Cherry Coke Barbecue Sauce.

Homemade Ranch Dressing

DIFFICULTY

MAKES ABOUT 1½ CUPS
PREP TIME: 10 MINUTES

¼ cup buttermilk

¼ cup heavy cream

½ cup mayonnaise
(I love Duke's)

½ cup sour cream

1 tablespoon dill
pickle juice

1 (0.4-ounce) packet
Hidden Valley Ranch
dressing mix

2 tablespoons
fresh parsley,
finely chopped

4 chives, finely
chopped

2 sprigs fresh dill,
finely chopped

1 small clove garlic,
minced (optional)

¼ teaspoon hot
sauce (optional)

Kosher salt, to taste

Freshly ground black
pepper, to taste

For when you're feeling a little bit fancy and want to go the extra mile to impress your guests, I suggest trying this homemade ranch dressing from the restaurant. It adds that extra little kick that will take your meal to the next level. Thanks, Chef Kurtess!

1. Place buttermilk, heavy cream, mayonnaise, sour cream, pickle juice, dressing mix, parsley, chives, dill, garlic (if using), and hot sauce (if using) in a large mixing bowl. Whisk gently until combined. Add salt and pepper to taste.

2. Pour the dressing into an airtight container and keep refrigerated for up to 1 week.

Nikki Spalaris's White-Chocolate Cranberry Cookies

MAKES 2 DOZEN COOKIES
PREP TIME: 20 MINUTES
COOK TIME: 10 MINUTES

DIFFICULTY

2 cups (4 sticks) salted butter, at room temperature

1 cup granulated sugar

4 cups all-purpose flour

1 cup white chocolate chips

1 cup dried cranberries (or dried cherries)

Nikki has been coming to my house to give me a mani-pedi and massage for eleven years. She started bringing these cookies over, and they've become a total hit with my family and friends. I'm so thankful to Nikki for her friendship, generosity, and delicious recipes!

1. Preheat the oven to 350°F. Line 2 baking sheets with parchment paper or silicone baking mats.

2. Place the butter and sugar in the bowl of an electric stand mixer or a large mixing bowl. Beat on medium-high speed until light and fluffy, about 4 to 5 minutes.

3. Turn the mixer to medium-low and add the flour one cup at a time, waiting until each addition is incorporated before adding the next, until the ingredients are combined.

4. Add the white chocolate chips and dried cranberries and mix to incorporate.

5. Place the dough by 2 tablespoon spoonfuls onto the cookie sheets, spacing them at least 1 inch apart. Transfer to the middle rack of the oven.

6. Bake for 10 to 14 minutes, until the cookies are golden brown on the edges. Remove the baking sheets from the oven.

7. Allow the cookies to rest on the sheets for 10 minutes, then transfer to a wire rack to cool completely before serving.

4

Curious People Are the Best People

I was a total scaredy-cat as a kid, easily the most cautious of the four of us kids. I hated to go out alone in the dark, and even one scary movie would have me lying awake night after night, eyes wide open and my blankets up under my neck in a death grip. My overactive imagination was just too dang good at convincing me to play it safe. Whenever it was my night to go turn the horses out at the barn, I'd always get Susie to go with me. Thank God she never said no!

I was also terrified of heights. We had an old barn with a lean-to attached where Daddy would put the sick yearlings to recover. Pake tied a rope from the rafters, and he and Alice would scramble up to the top and swing out over the hayloft to land on the mountain of loose hay below. They hollered like it was just the most fun they'd ever had. I desperately

53

wanted to do it too, but whenever I climbed up to the rope, my brain would conjure up pictures of all the ways I could hurt myself or that a snake might be down there in the hay, just waiting for me. I never did bring myself to take the leap.

A healthy sense of fear is helpful, but fear can also stop us from going after the things we want in life.

When Mama first talked to Red Steagall about my career after that life-changing moment when he heard me sing the national anthem, she actually pitched him the idea of signing our trio—the Singing McEntires, consisting of Pake, myself, and Susie (Alice didn't sing with us that much). Red didn't think he could take on all three of us kids, but he was interested in taking me to Nashville to record a demo. I wanted it so badly, but I also loved performing with Pake and Susie. That was my comfort zone. I was used to my rodeo family and my family at home. The music industry was something I knew nothing about.

Mama was the one who drove me all the way to Nashville. She could tell something was wrong because I kept suggesting we stop for ice cream, food, and every tourist trap along the way. I knew what a big opportunity this was, but I didn't know if I was ready to leave my siblings behind.

Finally, Mama said, "Now Reba, let me tell you something. If you don't want to go to Nashville, we don't have to do this. We can turn around and go right back home. But if you do this, I'll be living my dreams through you." I said, "Well, why didn't you say that in the first place? Let's go."

Thank God Mama gave me some perspective on what a once-in-a-lifetime chance this was. Home would always be there for me, but I was in the middle of a real-life fairy-tale moment. I couldn't give that up because of a little fear. I needed to root myself in something bigger.

The flip side of fear isn't fearlessness. It's curiosity. There's no magic switch to make you unafraid, but curiosity has a way of pushing us past our fears to say yes to the things that could be good for us.

In 1999, the producers of *Annie Get Your Gun* asked my agent if I'd be interested in playing Annie Oakley on Broadway. I politely turned them down because I was booked up touring South America, Australia, and Europe. I was roaming the world, and I didn't really want to sit in one place like you do on Broadway. Plus, I had my band and crew to think about.

Then one day in 2000, we were on our way to Europe and our flight got canceled. We found ourselves on a layover in New York City. Not a bad place to be! We decided to go see *Annie Get Your Gun* to check out what all the excitement was about.

I loved it. It had the best songs, humor and heart, happy moments and sad ones too—all the elements of a great country song. I'd always been a huge fan of Annie Oakley even before I was old enough to go to school. I loved Bernadette Peters and the rest of the cast! So we worked it out, and I took over the role of Annie in January 2001. The part really seemed like it had been written just for me. I'd always loved Annie's story, and I felt like I'd been born to play her.

I shadowed Cheryl Ladd, who played Annie before I did, and she really helped me out a lot. A Broadway play functions like a well-oiled machine, and it was my job to jump in and not miss a beat. I rehearsed from January 2nd to January 23rd, but I only got one dress rehearsal before my opening night, so I was learning on my feet. My publicist, Pete Sanders, had warned me not to look too closely at the reviews from opening night. "It's nothing personal. You just never know what the critics will say." But I wasn't worried about it. My dream to play Annie Oakley had already come true, and no critic in the whole world could take that away from me.

When I was doing press for the show, one reporter asked me whether I was scared to do Broadway since I'd never even been in a play before. I just looked at him kinda funny and said, "Shoot! I didn't even think about that!" Ignorance really is bliss sometimes! I was honestly so busy performing that I couldn't bother to worry. That role fit me like a glove, and I swear I had a new favorite song every night.

We did eight shows a week. It was the hardest job I ever had. I really did have to stay present and stay curious to make it feel fresh for the audience. I felt a little like Bill Murray in *Groundhog Day* some nights. I'd get halfway through a show and wonder if I'd already said that line.

Top Left: Celebrating my birthday backstage during the run of Annie Get Your Gun, 2001

Top Right: In the wings with my costar and good friend John Schuck, playing the role of Buffalo Bill, 2001

Bottom: Larry Storch, John Schuck, and me visiting with president George H. W. Bush and Barbara Bush after the show, 2001

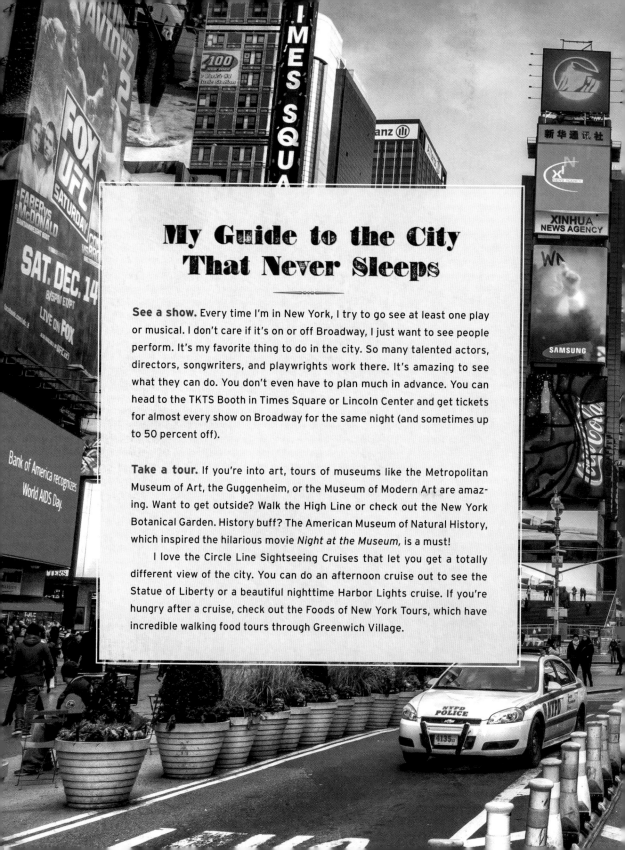

My Guide to the City That Never Sleeps

See a show. Every time I'm in New York, I try to go see at least one play or musical. I don't care if it's on or off Broadway, I just want to see people perform. It's my favorite thing to do in the city. So many talented actors, directors, songwriters, and playwrights work there. It's amazing to see what they can do. You don't even have to plan much in advance. You can head to the TKTS Booth in Times Square or Lincoln Center and get tickets for almost every show on Broadway for the same night (and sometimes up to 50 percent off).

Take a tour. If you're into art, tours of museums like the Metropolitan Museum of Art, the Guggenheim, or the Museum of Modern Art are amazing. Want to get outside? Walk the High Line or check out the New York Botanical Garden. History buff? The American Museum of Natural History, which inspired the hilarious movie *Night at the Museum,* is a must!

I love the Circle Line Sightseeing Cruises that let you get a totally different view of the city. You can do an afternoon cruise out to see the Statue of Liberty or a beautiful nighttime Harbor Lights cruise. If you're hungry after a cruise, check out the Foods of New York Tours, which have incredible walking food tours through Greenwich Village.

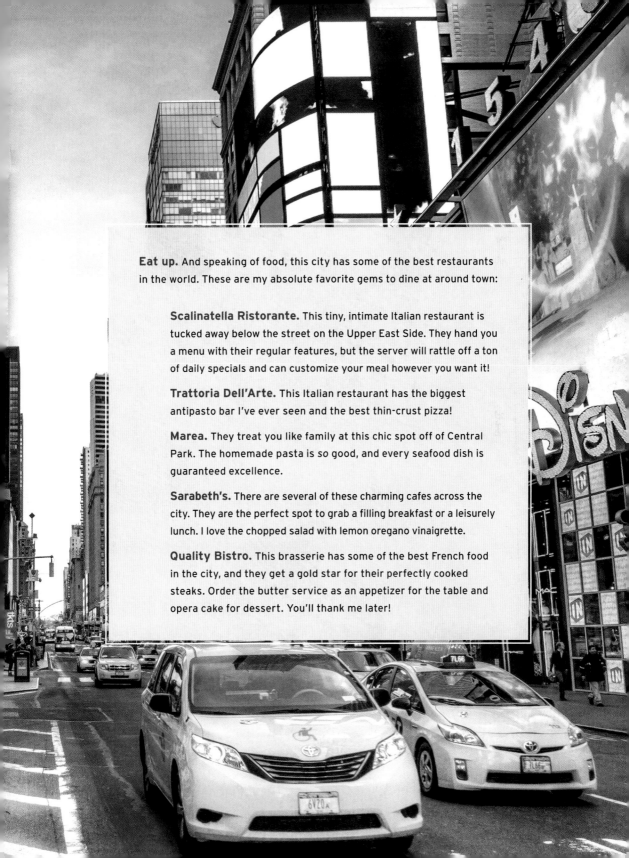

Eat up. And speaking of food, this city has some of the best restaurants in the world. These are my absolute favorite gems to dine at around town:

Scalinatella Ristorante. This tiny, intimate Italian restaurant is tucked away below the street on the Upper East Side. They hand you a menu with their regular features, but the server will rattle off a ton of daily specials and can customize your meal however you want it!

Trattoria Dell'Arte. This Italian restaurant has the biggest antipasto bar I've ever seen and the best thin-crust pizza!

Marea. They treat you like family at this chic spot off of Central Park. The homemade pasta is *so* good, and every seafood dish is guaranteed excellence.

Sarabeth's. There are several of these charming cafes across the city. They are the perfect spot to grab a filling breakfast or a leisurely lunch. I love the chopped salad with lemon oregano vinaigrette.

Quality Bistro. This brasserie has some of the best French food in the city, and they get a gold star for their perfectly cooked steaks. Order the butter service as an appetizer for the table and opera cake for dessert. You'll thank me later!

And I did mess up a few times. One night I was waiting for my entrance stage right while my costars Larry Storch and John Schuck were onstage together, when all of a sudden—silence. That's never a good thing in the theater. I looked up and saw John dressed as Buffalo Bill looking right at me. *Oh no, that's my line!* I burst onto the stage as if nothing had happened, and I picked up right where they left off. I'm not sure if the audience noticed, but John and I certainly did. That's going to happen when you're doing so many shows.

Even though it was the hardest job I'd ever had, it was also wonderful and challenging. I'll be honest, I wasn't sure how the Broadway community would react to a country girl like me, but I had forgotten that most actors and actresses aren't actually from New York City anyway. Many of them come from little towns just like I did, and the Broadway community couldn't have been more welcoming.

I find most creative folks will welcome you in as long as you come with some passion and curiosity.

Take the eighties, when MTV crashed onto the scene and popularized the concept of the music video. MCA and I split the cost to make a video for "Whoever's in New England," a song that songwriter Don Lanier and I discovered together. (Fun fact: when we chose that song, we initially assumed there might not be many country fans up in New England, but boy, were we wrong! We had more fan-club members in the Northeast than we did in the state of Texas!)

Striking a pose on set at the "Whoever's in New England" music video shoot, 1986

One afternoon in a hotel room while I was out on tour, I was watching HBO. Right after the movie ended, they played Aretha Franklin's latest video, and right after that, they played my video for "Whoever's in New England." I thought I'd died and gone to heaven! From then on, music videos became the standard for every single I released. My videos were like little mini-movies, definitely longer than what you see on social media today, but I really liked that. They allowed me just enough time to sink my teeth into a role and really get to know a character, and I realized I wanted to do more of that in my career.

At the time, very few country singers also acted—outside of the phenomenal Kenny Rogers, Kris Kristofferson, Mac Davis, Larry Gatlin, Johnny Cash, and Dolly Parton. So I talked to my agent about it and started reading scripts. I landed my first film role in *Tremors*, and more roles followed in films and made-for-television specials like *The Gambler Returns*, *North*, *One Night at McCool's*, and *The Little Rascals*. After that, I auditioned for television shows and eventually landed the part of Reba Hart on the TV show *Reba*.

I dreamed a lot of dreams growing up, but never in my wildest dreams could I have imagined a network show named after me. Just goes to show how important it is to stay open, stay curious, and keep trying something new. You never know what good thing is just around the corner.

You can't say yes to everything, but if it helps, I've figured out a pretty straightforward test for when to take a job. Just one simple question: *Is it fun?* If it's not fun, I don't want to do it.

So go on and say yes to those things you want, especially the stuff that makes your stomach turn somersaults or leaves you feeling a little breathless. That thing you've been dreaming of forever? It's time to take the leap—just steer clear of snakes.

Whole Lotta Hart

By Melissa Peterman (Barbra Jean)

Reba is who she is, whether wearing head-to-toe sequins, in full glam onstage, or on her back porch in jeans and a ball cap, no makeup, freckles out. She's warm, funny, down-to-earth, genuine, and authentic. It can be intimidating to meet Reba. I mean, there aren't many people the world knows by only one name! But that worry lasts for only about two seconds before Reba puts you at ease.

From day one, Reba fostered an atmosphere of fun on the set of *Reba*. We all felt a freedom to play built on a foundation of respect and gratitude for every individual's contribution. No one's job was more important than another. When people feel valued and secure, it's much easier to laugh, and Reba led the way in making sure we felt that way.

Reba is always up for a laugh, and she usually said yes when one of us asked her to participate in one of our silly ideas on set. Our prop masters, Jim Falkenstein and Gordie Germaine, are two of the funniest guys ever. Back in 2003, when Fountains of Wayne's "Stacy's Mom" was a huge hit, they got Reba to make a video with their version, "Shelby's Mom," with our cast and crew. Like I said, up for anything.

My son, Riley, on set giving Reba some genius notes to include more Barbra Jean in the script, Los Angeles, California, 2006

Reba and me on set for "The Pageant of Grandmas" episode, which featured both of our real-life moms, Jackie and Pam, Los Angeles, California, 2005

Reba enjoying a hug from me on set—she loves it, Los Angeles, California, 2002

The whole Reba cast—Scarlett Pomers, me, Chris Rich, Reba, JoAnna Garcia Swisher, Steve Howey, and Mitch Holleman—shooting our "Thanksgiving" episode, Los Angeles, California, 2004

Throughout the years, the cast and crew took several vacations together, including to Catalina Island, Mexico, Ireland, and on a cruise. And I won't lie, the idea of vacationing with my boss was scary that first time. *What if I spill my drink? Or swear? Say the wrong thing? Will my husband, John, be too loud? Will we both be too much?* The answer to all those questions is yes. But it never mattered, and a lot of that is because Reba set the tone. She would do something the first night to break the ice—usually a game around the dinner table, asking questions, sharing stories, laughing, getting to know each other. After that, we were off and running. My favorite moments traveling with Reba are always around a table, playing games, usually in PJs, sipping cocktails, eating snacks, and laughing.

Across our six-season run, our cast and crew shared a ton of life milestones together. I don't know how many, but lots of babies were born, including my son, Riley. We watched each other's families grow and shared our real families with our show family. Sharing those milestone moments bonds you together, and Reba and I never stopped sharing them, even after the show ended. It's hard to pinpoint the moment I realized that Reba was going to be in my life for the long haul, but when you start to share the things in life that aren't fun, it's clear who you can count on. When there's heartbreak, divorce, sadness, and loss, it matters who has your back. I know Reba has mine, and she knows I have hers. Always.

Chris Rich's Chicken and Vegetables

MAKES 4 SERVINGS
PREP TIME: 20 MINUTES
COOK TIME: 50 MINUTES

DIFFICULTY

2 tablespoons olive oil

4 to 6 fingerling potatoes, scrubbed and cut in half lengthwise

1 large sweet potato, scrubbed and roughly chopped

1 small yellow onion, roughly chopped

1 small red onion, roughly chopped

1 yellow bell pepper, cut into 1-inch strips, then halved

1 green bell pepper, cut into 1-inch strips, then halved

1 red bell pepper, cut into 1-inch strips, then halved

1 cup fresh green beans, ends removed

4 to 6 cloves garlic, minced (or as many cloves as you want—I like a lot!)

1 cup baby carrots

1 cup broccoli florets

1 cup cauliflower florets

Kosher salt, to taste

Freshly ground black pepper, to taste

4 bone-in skin-on chicken breasts

¼ cup salted butter, cubed

½ cup dry white wine

Chris played my ex-husband on *Reba*, and he's an excellent cook! Sometimes before a table read, I'd talk him into making me a breakfast sandwich or whatever he was eating at the time. It was always so good! Thanks, Chris, for always sharing and for teaching me how to cook vegetables!

1. Preheat the oven to 400°F. Drizzle the olive oil over the bottom of a large roasting pan.

2. Add the vegetables to the pan and toss to coat in the oil. Season liberally with salt and pepper.

3. Pat the chicken breasts dry and season liberally on all sides with salt and pepper. Arrange them evenly on top of the vegetables.

4. Scatter the cubed butter evenly over the chicken and vegetables. Pour the wine into the pan. Transfer to the middle rack of the oven.

5. Roast for 45 to 55 minutes, stirring the vegetables halfway through, until the potatoes are tender and chicken is golden brown with an internal temperature of 165°F.

6. Remove the pan from the oven. Allow to rest for 5 minutes, then serve.

You can substitute or exclude any of these vegetables. Just make sure you have roughly the same amount of colorful vegetables. It makes the dish look—and taste—better!

Reba's Mexican Cornbread

MAKES 16 SERVINGS
PREP TIME: 20 MINUTES
COOK TIME: 30 MINUTES

DIFFICULTY

1 tablespoon salted butter

1 medium sweet onion, chopped

1 pound lean ground beef or turkey

½ teaspoon kosher salt

1 teaspoon Reba's Place Burger Seasoning (p. 121)

2 (8.5-ounce) packages Jiffy Corn Muffin Mix

2 eggs

2/3 cup whole milk

8 slices American cheese

1 (14.75-ounce) can creamed corn

I've never been considered much of a cook. But when I make my beans and Mexican cornbread, no one ever complains! As my daughter, Chass, would say, "She loves beans!" True, and I love my Mexican cornbread too!

1. Preheat the oven to 400°F. Spray a 9 x 13-inch baking dish with nonstick cooking spray.

2. Melt the butter in a large frying pan over medium-high heat. Add the onion and sauté until softened and translucent.

3. Add the ground meat to the pan. Cook, breaking up the meat with a spatula, until thoroughly browned. Season with salt and Reba's Place Burger Seasoning (if using). Carefully drain any excess fat from the pan and set aside.

4. Place the cornbread mix in a large mixing bowl. Add the eggs and milk and whisk until combined.

5. Pour half of the cornbread batter into the baking dish. Sprinkle evenly with the browned meat and onion mixture. Arrange the American cheese slices over the meat.

6. Mix the creamed corn into the remaining cornbread batter. Pour the mixture into the baking dish, covering the layer of cheese. Transfer to the middle rack of the oven.

7. Bake for 25 to 30 minutes, or until a toothpick inserted in the center comes out clean.

8. Remove the baking dish from the oven. Allow to cool for at least 30 minutes before serving.

"Whoever's in New England" Mule

DIFFICULTY

MAKES 1 DRINK
PREP TIME: 5 MINUTES

1½ ounces whiskey

½ ounce cranberry juice

½ ounce freshly
squeezed orange juice

¼ ounce grenadine

Dash of salt

1 (6.8-ounce) bottle
ginger beer

1 slice orange, for garnish

2 luxardo cherries,
for garnish

While your special someone is up there with whoever's in New England, I recommend kicking back and having a few of these.

1. Fill a copper mule mug with ice. Pour in the whiskey, cranberry juice, orange juice, and grenadine. Sprinkle in the dash of salt and stir to mix.

2. Top the drink off with ginger beer. Garnish with the orange slice and cherries. Enjoy!

5

You Gotta Be You

Back when I was starting out, women weren't getting the respect male singers got. Dolly Parton, Tammy Wynette, Loretta Lynn, and Barbara Mandrell certainly broke through barriers and paved a smoother road for all of us who followed. But that didn't mean it was easy.

They used to introduce me as "The little girl singer, Reba McEntire." These days, you'd be castrated for saying that, but that's just how it was back then. I wasn't offended. I *was* a girl singer. But I was very frustrated that I couldn't call the shots myself. I knew the boys in the business were all picking their own songs and producers and running their tours the way they wanted to. Why couldn't I?

Then one day, my producer, Jerry Kennedy, played me a song called "Can't Even Get the Blues." It was up-tempo, sassy, and strong—a real departure from the waltzes I'd been recording. I loved it from the first moment I heard it, but he'd intended it for Jacky Ward, my fellow labelmate.

"Why wouldn't you pitch me a song like that?" I asked him.

"You'd record that?"

"You bet!"

So we did. It became the second single on *Unlimited*, my fifth album, and it went to number one. It was great to feel like I had a seat at the table for what I wanted my career to be.

In 1984, I left PolyGram/Mercury Records, although I will be forever grateful to everyone there—Jerry Kennedy, Frank Lefel, and the whole team—for how they took a chance on me back when I was just starting out. I found my way over to MCA Records. After I had been there a while, I expressed how I wanted to do an album like the ones I'd grown up with, complete with fiddles and steel guitars instead of an orchestra. Jimmy Bowen, my producer and head of the label, said, "Well, woman. Go find your own songs then."

Find them myself? That was music to my ears. Don Lanier and I went from publishing company to publishing company looking for old-school country songs like the ones I'd been raised on. Songs that told stories and tugged on your heartstrings.

We met with Harlan Howard, a famous songwriter who had written hits for Patsy Cline, Buck Owens, and many others. He was brilliant, and I thought surely we could make something work. So we paid him a visit and listened to his songs. Now, I didn't want to offend Mr. Howard, but they just weren't what I was looking for. No goosebumps, no little shiver up my spine. Nothing.

So I told him I was passing on them. I think he was testing me. Only after I turned down those songs did he play me "Somebody Should Leave." It was the saddest country song I'd ever heard, and I wanted it. It became the centerpiece of *My Kind of Country* and went to number one. That was the album that helped turn me from a singer into an artist.

There's no handbook for how to find a hit, and those years going out and choosing my songs really taught me how to trust my gut instincts. I learned not to overthink it too much. If you're moved by it, just trust that the listeners will be moved also. My gut hasn't steered me wrong yet.

Trusting your gut doesn't mean choosing blindly. It means doing your research and surrounding yourself with a team you can trust. It means getting in the right rooms and doing your best to collaborate with people who love what they do just as much as you do.

I started out in the music industry knowing less than nothing about the business, and I mostly could have just stayed that way. Instead, I learned everything I could from the experts around me. I'm so grateful to my record labels and managers Don Williams, Bill Carter, Narvel Blackstock, and Clarence Spalding. I looked up to performers like Red Steagall, Tom T. Hall, the Statler Brothers, Conway Twitty, Mel Tillis, Mickey Gilley, and Ronnie Milsap. I was also mentored by music

Okie Party Playlist

Oklahoma breeds stars. Good ones too. One Garth Brooks concert was so loud that it registered as an earthquake! *That's* an Oklahoma boy who knows how to shake up a crowd. Here's a playlist of some fellow Oklahomans to get your party started:

- ★ "Oklahoma Swing" by Vince Gill
- ★ "Callin' Baton Rouge" by Garth Brooks
- ★ "Amazing Grace" by Carrie Underwood
- ★ "Ol' Red" by Blake Shelton
- ★ "Right or Wrong" by Wanda Jackson
- ★ "Before He Cheats" by Carrie Underwood
- ★ "Because He Lives" by Kristin Chenoweth
- ★ "As Good as I Once Was" by Toby Keith
- ★ "When I Call Your Name" by Vince Gill
- ★ "I Want a Cowboy" by Katrina Elam
- ★ "Thank God and Greyhound" by Roy Clark
- ★ "Prop Me Up Beside the Jukebox (If I Die)" by Joe Diffie
- ★ "Go Rest High on That Mountain" by Vince Gill
- ★ "How Great Thou Art" by Carrie Underwood
- ★ "The Beaches of Cheyenne" by Garth Brooks
- ★ "Back in the Saddle Again" by Gene Autry
- ★ "Baby's Got Her Blue Jeans On" by Mel McDaniel
- ★ "I'm a Woman" by Kristin Chenoweth
- ★ "I Still Believe in You" by Vince Gill

industry pros like my producers Jerry Kennedy, Norro Wilson, Jimmy Bowen, Buddy Cannon, Tony Brown, David Malloy, Dann Huff, and Dave Cobb. Thanks to their guidance and advice, I found my way one baby step at a time.

I always tried to keep an open mind about others' opinions. I wanted to stay receptive to any advice that would help my career. I listened, and then I ran it all through a gut check. If it felt right, I used it. If it didn't, well, I tried something different. I'm grateful to all the people who were willing to give me advice and guidance, even if I didn't always do what they suggested. There are so many people to thank. I wouldn't be where I am today without all of them.

For instance, we wouldn't have the *Revived Remixed Revisited* box set without Justin McIntosh and my record label, Universal Music Group, who came up with the idea. On *Revived*, my band and I rerecorded some of my classic songs the way we performed them onstage. *Remixed* was a group of songs we selected to record as dance mixes. And for *Revisited*, Dave Cobb recorded ten songs of mine as stripped-back acoustic versions. Each album is completely different, and I love them all.

Part of the reasoning behind doing this box set was to introduce my music to some of the younger generations of my fans who are active on platforms like TikTok. We love TikTok. I get a kick out of it. Mama always said I have the attention span of a two-year-old, so TikTok's perfect for me.

I like watching my fans reimagining my music. There was one trend where people lip-synced along to "I'm a Survivor" while acting out basic tasks, like taking out the trash

or making a sandwich. That tickled me to pieces. There was even one person sitting on the toilet seat replacing the toilet paper roll. So funny!

Before social media, you put out music and then met fans at shows or at events, but you didn't get to see them connect with your music in their daily lives. Now, thanks to TikTok and other social media platforms, I get to watch my fans interpret my music in their own ways. I've never felt more connected to my fans, and I love it.

Story behind the Song:
"The Night the Lights Went Out in Georgia"

Back in 1972, Bobby Russell went all over town trying to get someone to sing this new song he'd written. A lot of famous artists turned him down, but he thought they were making a huge mistake.

"I *know* this is a hit," he told everyone. "Even my wife could sing this song and make it a hit!" You know what people said? "Let her."

So his wife, Vicki Lawrence—a phenomenally funny actress from *The Carol Burnett Show,* who also went on to star in the popular *Mama's Family*—took on that challenge. It was her one and only number one song in the US: "The Night the Lights Went Out in Georgia." I loved it so much that I recorded it myself almost twenty years later. Again, it just goes to show you, sometimes you have to trust your gut.

For the music video, I had to age from sixteen years old to eighty-two. The makeup department needed to make a mold of my face for the prosthetic wrinkles, so one day I had to sit still in a chair for a few hours while they put plaster on my face with straws sticking out of my nose so I could breathe. Not my most glamorous moment, but I do think it was worth it in the end! I still perform "The Night the Lights Went Out in Georgia" on tour today. When the first chord of that song hits, the crowd goes wild.

Sitting down with my good friend Vicki Lawrence on her popular talk show, Vicki!, 1994

Nashville Hot Chicken

DIFFICULTY

MAKES 4 TO 6 SERVINGS
PREP TIME: 25 MINUTES
COOK TIME: 45 MINUTES
INACTIVE TIME: 24 HOURS

SEASONING MIX

2 tablespoons cayenne pepper

2 tablespoons sweet paprika

1 tablespoon granulated garlic

1 tablespoon brown
sugar, packed

1 tablespoon kosher salt

CHICKEN

12 pieces bone-in skin-on
chicken breasts, thighs,
legs, and wings (or cut
your own whole chicken)

2 cups buttermilk, plus
more if needed

1 gallon peanut oil (or
vegetable oil), for frying

2 cups all-purpose
flour, divided

1 teaspoon kosher salt, divided

4 egg whites

1/3 cup water

1 cup masa harina (also called
"corn masa" or "corn flour")

1 cup cracker meal
or matzo meal

1 teaspoon freshly
ground black pepper

Sliced white bread and dill
pickle slices, for serving

Nashville is known for hot chicken. So it seemed natural to include it on the menu at my restaurant. Ain't no hot like Nashville hot, but if you like it a little milder, use less cayenne. Like I said, you gotta be you.

SEASONING MIX

1. Place the cayenne, sweet paprika, garlic, brown sugar, and salt in a wide-mouthed glass jar and secure the lid. Shake to combine.

CHICKEN

1. Place the chicken in a large mixing bowl and pour in the buttermilk. Make sure the chicken is fully submerged. Cover the bowl with plastic wrap and refrigerate for 24 hours.

2. Attach a thermometer to the side of a large Dutch oven and add the peanut oil. Heat the oil to 350°F and maintain the temperature within a range of 25°F. Line a baking sheet with parchment paper and set it next to the Dutch oven. Set a cooling rack on top of a second baking sheet and place it next to the Dutch oven.

3. Place 1 cup of flour and $1/2$ teaspoon of salt in a shallow bowl. Whisk to combine. In a second bowl, whisk together the egg whites and water until lightly frothy. Place the remaining 1 cup of flour, masa harina, cracker meal, remaining $1/2$ teaspoon of salt, and pepper in a third shallow bowl. Whisk to combine.

4. Lift a piece of chicken from the buttermilk and shake off the excess. Dredge the chicken in the bowl of flour, turning to coat all sides, then submerge in the egg whites. Allow the excess to drip back into the bowl, then transfer to the cracker mixture. Press gently to adhere the breading and flip to coat both sides. Transfer the chicken to the baking sheet. Repeat with the remaining pieces.

5. Fry the chicken 3 to 4 pieces at a time until the coating is deeply golden brown and the meat reaches an internal temperature of 165°F, about 12 to 15 minutes. Carefully lift the chicken from the oil using a deep fryer skimmer and transfer to the cooling rack.

6. Once all the chicken is fried, place the Seasoning Mix in a large mixing bowl. Add $1/2$ cup of the hot frying oil to the bowl and whisk to combine. Add the fried chicken to the bowl and toss until evenly coated.

7. Arrange sliced white bread in a single layer on a serving platter and place the fried chicken on top. Top with dill pickle slices and serve immediately.

*Rex and me enjoying golden hour at
the Celebrity Adventures retreat,
Brush Creek Ranch, Wyoming*

Sunday Kind of Love

I'm all about a not-that-fancy date. Here are some of my favorite date-night ideas that guarantee a good time for you and your bank account:

★ **At-Home Dinner and a Movie.** Plan a fun dinner menu from this book, and serve it by candlelight! Afterward, snuggle up on the couch under a cozy blanket and watch an old classic or a new-to-you movie.

★ **Picnic in the Park.** We love going on a hike. Here in Nashville, Percy Warner Park offers great trails with the prettiest views. For lunch, pack your own basket or pick up sandwiches from your favorite spot. Just make sure to pack cold drinks and bug spray!

★ **Get Competitive.** Break out a set of cards or your favorite board games and play a few rounds. Make it even more interesting by placing bets.

★ **Hit the Road.** Nothing makes you feel like a teenager again like driving around with no destination in mind. Blast the music, roll down the windows, and pull off on the side of the road to take a look at the stars.

We have "Coffee Camp" together every morning. Whether we're together in person or far apart talking on the phone, we make sure we spend quality time together before we start our day. Sometimes when I have early-morning TV shows and I'm in Nashville and he's in L.A., those coffee calls are more like pre-dawn calls for Rex. But he never complains. He's always happy to hear from me, and starting my day with Rex always sets me on a path toward a great mood. He's the first person I talk to when I get up each morning and the last person I talk to before I go to sleep each night.

I'm having fun being in love again. Romantic relationships should be fun—I don't care how old you are. Love should bring you joy and laughter and make you feel good, and I'm never going to settle for anything less.

show instead. Afterward I was sick for about three weeks because of the stress. Garth Brooks, whether you know it or not, you pushed me out of my comfort zone! Thanks for that! Love ya!

One of my favorite annual competitions happens at Red Steagall's Roundup, an annual Montana trip. We go up for a week of riding, singing, playing games, eating, and visiting. We have a blast! One of my favorite contests is called Team Pinning. It's played in an arena. On one end of the arena, a team made up of three riders enters on horseback. On the other end, twelve head of cattle are waiting, each with a number painted on its back. Someone calls out three numbers, and the riders have to herd the corresponding cattle into a holding pen on the other end of the arena. Fastest time wins. It can get a little Western out there, to put it mildly. The way we all holler and cheer and carry on, you'd think there was a big pot of prize money, but really, we're all just in it for bragging rights. Red and I won Team Pinning one year, and the next time we were there, Rex and I won. The other contest we love is mounted shooting. More on that later.

Left: Red and me celebrating our Team Pinning win, Montana, 2018

Right: Fist bumping Rex after our big win, Montana, 2020

At the end of the day, I love to compete with my friends, whether in a rodeo arena, from the rafters, or on a ranch. It's fun to get a little dirty and try something new, especially when you're surrounded by people you care about. I really like to win—trust me, I do—but with good folks like these in my life, I feel like I've already won.

Game On!

We McEntires have always been partial to playing games. Monopoly was Pake's favorite when we were growing up. He could always charm Susie and me into a game. Of course, once we started playing, he wouldn't let us quit until he'd won. You can bet Susie and I did everything we could to make sure Pake won after four hours of playing!

Here are some of my current favorite indoor and outdoor games to play with family and friends these days.

---

* **Cornhole.** Everyone from little ones to old-timers can enjoy this toss game! If you live in the South, you're bound to know someone with a cornhole board who can bring theirs along to the party. Or if you're feeling fancy, you can have one custom-made featuring your favorite team logo or your family's monogram. And the best part is, you can toss with one hand and hold your drink in another.

* **Rummikub.** This mix of mah-jongg and gin rummy is so fun and addictive. It can keep you busy and having fun for hours.

* **Horseshoes.** This is one of the simplest games to set up, especially if you live on a ranch or a farm. All you need is a pole of some sort and a handful of horseshoes. If you want to get a little fancy, paint the shoes in different colors so each player can identify their own.

* **Skyjo.** This card game is fun for all ages. Unlike other games, it's the player with the lowest score who wins! Thanks Calamity, Chism, and Autumn for introducing us to this and Rummikub.

* **Backgammon.** I learned how to play this popular two-person game while on vacation with president George H. W. Bush and Barbara Bush, and it quickly became one of my favorites. It's also one of the oldest table games in existence.

* **Monopoly.** Just not with Pake!

Pepper—the judge—and our friend Jamie assuming the role of the Hot Pepper—the Great Pepper's assistant. It was a whole lot of fun just hanging out, eating, and laughing silly. At the end of the day, sure enough, Shane was the winner. But what I don't understand is why his recipe left out the beans! Hmm?! Playing to the judge, Shane? We decided to call the shindig the "Hillbilly Chili Cook-Off at the Fork," and we have made a tradition out of it.

Marci and Nathan posing with their participation trophies, 2022

Shelby and Marissa joining in the fun, 2022

The Great Pepper deep in thought, 2022

Matt "Catfish" Johnson winning Best Dressed at the first Chili Cook-Off, 2022

Shane "Wild West" Tarleton's Winning Chili

MAKES 6 TO 8 SERVINGS
PREP TIME: 30 MINUTES
COOK TIME: 2½ HOURS

DIFFICULTY

Shane's no chef and—full disclosure—he said he tried multiple concoctions before he landed this one successfully. But thanks to the Hillbilly Chili Cook-Off, we know it's a winner!

2 pounds chuck roast beef, cut into 1-inch cubes

Kosher salt

Black pepper

3 tablespoons ghee (or unsalted butter), divided

1 large yellow onion, chopped

2 cloves garlic, minced

1 tomato, chopped

1 (6-ounce) can tomato paste

1 tablespoon chili powder

1 tablespoon ancho chili powder (or additional chili powder)

1½ teaspoons paprika

1½ teaspoons cumin

Big pinch of cayenne pepper

½ small Carolina cayenne pepper, seeded and finely chopped (optional for very hot chili)

1½ cups water

½ cup spicy Bloody Mary mix (optional)

1½ teaspoons hot sauce (Shane uses ¾ teaspoon each of Don Julio Salsa Picante and Valentina Salsa Picante)

1. Season the beef liberally with salt and pepper. Add 1 tablespoon of ghee to a large, wide-bottomed pot and set it over medium-high heat. Once hot, add half the beef. Sear, keeping the cubes spaced apart as much as possible, until browned on all sides, about 5 to 6 minutes. Transfer the cooked beef to a large bowl and repeat with another 1 tablespoon of ghee and the remaining cubed beef.

2. Add the remaining 1 tablespoon of ghee to the pot and add the onions. Cook, stirring frequently, until softened and lightly browned, about 5 to 6 minutes. Add the garlic and sauté just until fragrant.

Around My Table

I like everyone to be included. Whether I've known you since we were little or just met you five minutes ago, if you're at my table, I want you to feel right at home.

When you're at dinner with a group of people, it's easy for folks to pair off and keep discussion at their end of the table. I like to play a game that gets everyone at the table talking, especially if there are some newer faces in the group.

We start with me asking a question and everyone taking turns answering. Then whoever's sitting next to me gets to ask the next question and so on. It gets everyone talking, and you learn things about people that you wouldn't learn in a normal conversation. This game allows the quieter ones to have a chance to be heard. Here's my go-to list to get you started, but feel free to mix it up!

★ How old were you when you lost your virginity? (That's definitely an icebreaker!)

★ If you could have dinner with anybody, dead or alive, who would it be and why?

★ Cookies, cake, or pie? (Pro tip: write down the answer to this one so you're ready for that person's next birthday.)

★ Tell us about the most embarrassing thing that ever happened to you.

★ When were you last afraid and why?

★ When was the last time you laughed until you cried?

★ What is your favorite place on earth and why?

★ Who would you want to play you in a movie of your life?

★ Who makes you feel most at home?

★ If you could relive one day from your life, which day would it be and why?

★ What do you think other people value most about you? What do you value most about yourself?

★ If you were a TV show character, which existing show do you think you'd be on?

One show, during our last song of the night, we were standing close together, and Kix kept spraying me with spit as he sang. When we got offstage I hollered at him, "Would you stop spitting in my face?" Ronnie Dunn thought that was hilarious. The next night, when I arrived at my dressing room, I found a bright yellow raincoat with a hood and rain pants waiting for me. I'm not sure if it was Ronnie or Kix who sent it, but I loved it. Still, I couldn't let them have the last word. So when I went to change for the last song, Sandi had my rain gear ready. I put it on and went on up to perform. The look on Kix's face was priceless. We laughed about that raincoat for years to come.

Kix's Straight-Up Barbecue Sauce

DIFFICULTY

½ yellow onion, very finely chopped

2 cups ketchup

¼ cup light corn syrup

¼ cup dry red wine

1 tablespoon fresh lemon juice

1 tablespoon whole-grain spicy mustard

1½ teaspoons Worcestershire sauce

1 tablespoon brown sugar, packed

2 cloves garlic, grated

½ teaspoon kosher salt

¼ teaspoon cayenne pepper, more or less to taste

Hot sauce, to taste

What I like about this homemade barbecue sauce is that it's super easy to make, and you don't have to cook it. This recipe makes about 2½ cups, so double it if you think you'll need more sauce than that. This sauce would be great on any recipe calling for barbecue sauce; I especially like it with Kix's ribs.

1. Place the onion, ketchup, corn syrup, wine, lemon juice, mustard, Worcestershire, brown sugar, garlic, salt, cayenne, and hot sauce (if using) in a large mixing bowl. Whisk until smooth and combined.

2. Use immediately, or transfer to an airtight container and refrigerate for up to 1 week.

9

Betty

I'm proud to say that my brother and my sisters are three of my very best friends. They taught me what friendship was before I even had a word for it. Our friendship was born while pretending to be cowboys and cowgirls down at the ropin' pen and running outside singing "Anything You Can Do, I Can Do Better." And while singing along to Johnny Tillotson on Mama's old Motorola record player, using hairbrushes for microphones.

I'll never forget the time I came home from a basketball game and found that Susie and Pake had taken all the shoestrings out of every shoe in my closet and threaded them through some plastic hair rollers to booby-trap my room. I couldn't even walk in there! I couldn't get anywhere without getting caught up in it. I probably should have been mad, but instead I thought, *They took all that time to do that. They really like me.*

Pranks and joking around are some of my favorite things, which might have started from hanging with my brother, Pake. He's the only boy in the family, but he never treated us girls like we were delicate just because we were girls. We fought and wrestled and absolutely tore each other up.

Left: Pake, Alice, and me trying out a new style together, Chockie, Oklahoma, 1958

Right: Me watching Pake practice his roping skills at a rodeo, 1959

He tells a great story and has an amazing memory for dirty jokes. I won't repeat any of *those* here, but despite the dirty jokes, Pake has always been so protective of us three girls.

Pake still sings and plays the fiddle. When we were in the Singing McEntires, he'd sing lead and play guitar, and Susie and I sang harmony. He even went to Nashville and recorded an album. In the eighties, Pake had a recording contract with RCA Records and had a top-five record. But the music business just wasn't for him. He was always a rancher and rodeo cowboy at heart.

Pake and I used to haul together on the rodeo circuit for a while after I graduated from high school, pooling together our money to split

The Singing McEntires consisting of me, Pake, and Susie,, 1971

a chicken-fried steak to cut expenses. I have such fond memories of long drives and sharing rooms and celebrating wins together. He's always had my back, and he's always quick to make me laugh.

I'm every bit as close with my sisters. One of my most favorite things I got to do with Mama, Alice, and Susie was go on girls trips. We got to travel together several times and always had a blast. I'm

I brought her along on another trip where I was performing at a college that has this beautiful lake behind its campus. Marci just had her hair professionally blown out. She wanted to look her best for the trip since her crush, Jim Kimball, my guitar player, would be there. We were invited to swim in the lake, and Marci's crush thought that could be a lot of fun. "But your hair," I told her. Marci didn't care, and like I said, she's the kind of person who likes to say yes to fun things. So one of the lifeguards found her a bathing suit to borrow, and she got right in—borrowed bathing suit, ruined blowout, and all. But hey, she got the guy—still dating him today.

Without fail, no matter where we go, Marci gets everyone laughing and having fun because *she's* always laughing and having fun. We could go to a fancy hotel in Paris or the Motel Six in Myrtle Beach, and we'd have a fun adventure either way. But Marci says that what *really* defines our friendship is sitting on the back porch. Whether it's my back porch, looking out at the hills, horses, donkeys, and longhorns, or sitting on her back porch, watching her chickens run around, looking at her beautiful lakefront view, sitting and talking and just being ourselves with each other is what our friendship is all about.

I can't think of a single place in this world I couldn't go with Marci by my side.

Another close friend of mine is Shane Tarleton, a Warner music Nashville record executive I've been lucky enough to know for years. Shane can make me laugh, or we can discuss serious music business topics. I know I can call him whenever I need a pep talk, and he'll cheer me right up and give me that confidence boost I need. Of course, I'm always happy to return the favor. He's kind and generous, and when he's not working hard, you can find him giving back with organizations all over Nashville. He's a gem, and I'm lucky to have him in my corner.

Betty, the Hostess with the Mostest (Rhinestones, That Is)

By Marci

Betty loves to entertain and get people together. She makes even normal little trips or dinner or get-togethers into events. She just can't help herself. Not necessarily fancy events—those aren't as much her style—but funny, silly, or over-the-top events. And they are always memorable.

For example, Betty and Rex had planned our first annual chili cook-off. They had picked different winning categories, with first place going to the best overall chili. They found the perfect spot in Leiper's Fork and had shirts, hats, and wooden spoons made for everyone—the whole deal. I'd really been working on my chili and had several versions—a venison one and a few others. I was ready.

At the last minute, Betty decided we should have a Best-Dressed competition. I guess she figured her chili wouldn't be as good as everyone else's. She asked to borrow a pair of overalls because everyone was required to wear them to the competition. So I sent her down a pair of my old overalls to borrow for the weekend. They weren't anything special. Just some basic faded, light-wash overalls.

Well, I show up for the party, and—I'm not kidding—Betty had talked Neil Robison, who does her hair and makeup, into bedazzling those overalls for her. There were rhinestones everywhere—all along every single seam. She had them on over a gray-and-white leopard-print shirt with a bright purple scarf. I think she was thinking she'd win Best Dressed even if she didn't win first place for her chili. And after all that, she didn't even win! Catfish, Reba's property manager, did!

7. Bake for 15 to 18 minutes, until the cookies are golden brown on the edges. Remove the baking sheets from the oven.

8. Allow the cookies to rest on the sheets for 10 minutes, then transfer to a wire rack to cool completely before serving.

> This dough can be made 1 week in advance and frozen for up to 1 month. Store baked cookies in an airtight container at room temperature for 2 days, or in the refrigerator for 1 week.

Louis Calabro's Mint, Lemon, and Ginger Iced Tea

MAKES 4 SERVINGS
PREP TIME: 15 MINUTES
INACTIVE TIME: 8 HOURS

DIFFICULTY

6 cups filtered water

²/3 cup sugar

1 thumb-sized knob fresh ginger root, peeled and thinly sliced

1/2 cup fresh mint leaves, plus more for garnish

4 peppermint tea bags (or 4 tablespoons loose leaf peppermint tea)

1 cup fresh lemon juice

Sliced lemon, for garnish

As I mentioned, my friends and I love an iced tea. This one might not get you as tipsy as we were out there in Barbados, but it sure does taste a whole lot better. This is a re-creation of a recipe one of my friends, composer Louis Calabro, kindly brought to a party I had once. I usually double or triple this recipe and keep a pitcher chilled in the fridge for later.

1. Pour the water into a large saucepan and set over medium-high heat. Bring to a boil. Add the sugar and stir until dissolved.

2. Remove the pan from the heat. Add the ginger, mint, and tea. Allow to steep for 12 to 15 minutes, then strain into a pitcher through a fine mesh sieve.

3. Stir the lemon juice into the tea. Transfer to the refrigerator and chill until cold, at least 8 hours.

4. To serve, pour the tea into tall glasses of ice. Garnish with lemon slices and fresh mint leaves, and enjoy!

How to Say Good-bye

In an ideal world, we'd all have the chance to say good-bye to the people we love before they pass, but that doesn't always happen. That's why it's so important to tell our people how much we love them all the time.

* **Talk to those you've lost.** Say how you feel out loud. This will help you feel more connected to your lost loved ones, and it will help you process your grief. I believe that the ones who have gone on can hear me, so talking to them when I miss them always helps me feel better. Visit their old favorite spots, wherever you feel closest to them, and talk it out.

* **Honor them with what you do best.** This might be through your work or through creating art or through a hobby. Whatever you love to do, do it for them—like I sing now for Mama, as I always have.

* **Keep their memory alive.** Talk about the people you've lost. Reminisce about your favorite times and all the best things about them. Let yourself laugh about the funny stuff you did together. Look at old pictures and videos.

* **Give back.** Donate to a charity in their name, if you're able, or volunteer for an organization that they supported. Pay the love you have for them forward to others in need.

* **Set aside time to commemorate.** Holidays and other important days can be tough after a loss. Put aside some time during the day to reflect on and honor who you lost.

"You just say, 'Hi, Helen. It's Jac.' And then Helen will talk," I said. "It doesn't need to be complicated."

In times like that, when you can't find the words, all you really need to do is just keep each other company.

I do my best to check in with my friends regularly. I may not always have time for regular dinners or weekly visits, but even just a friendly text, a card on their birthday, or a phone call when I'm thinking about them goes a long way. Supporting your people might mean holding their hand at a funeral, dropping off a comforting meal, or just having them over to sit on the porch.

To my mama, my daddy, and all of those I love and miss, I'm still doing it for you. Thanks for having my back up there in heaven. And to my band that went on way too soon, I'm so grateful that God decided to put me with you for whatever time we had together in this lifetime. I'm looking forward to making more music with you up in heaven someday.

Jim Hammon

Back Row: Paula Kaye Evans, Michael Thomas, Joey Cigainero, Terry Jackson
Front Row: Kirk Cappello, Tony Saputo

Chris Austin

In Loving Memory

Build Your Own Crew

When you're a musician, you have to have a great crew. Having a good team around you can make life easier and help you grow. Each member brings their own specialties and strengths, and as a whole, you bring out the best in each other. Surround yourself with good folks who will support you, encourage you, and help you be the best you can be.

* **Drummer.** We all need someone who can help us keep the beat. This is a person who helps remind you of the important things in life and encourages you to keep your core values front and center.

* **Harmony Singers.** These are the peacekeepers in your life, the ones you never seem to fall out of sync with, no matter how long it's been since you saw them last. They inspire you to find calm when you are stressed.

* **Lead Guitarist.** This is your friend who helps you carry the melody. This isn't the friend you call to bail you out when you get into trouble; this is the friend who is sitting next to you laughing and saying, "Dang! That was fun!"

* **Manager.** This is the friend who tells it to you like it is and makes things happen. This is the go-getter who won't let you make excuses when it comes to the big (or small) things you want out of life.

* **Publicist.** This is the first person in line who is ready to celebrate your successes. They can take the sting out of your failures and help you put them into the proper context.

* **Songwriter.** We all need someone creative who makes the world a more beautiful place. This is the friend who helps you express your own creativity and dream big dreams for yourself.

* **Roadie.** This is the person in your life who you can count on for help, no matter what. They will always show up for you. There's no job too small.

Cherry Coke Barbecue Burger

MAKES 4 SERVINGS
PREP TIME: 15 MINUTES
COOK TIME: 10 MINUTES

DIFFICULTY

My band and I have spent a lot of time together on the road over the years. In the early years, when I was traveling on a bus, we ate in truck stops and fast-food joints, especially in the eighties. And that meant burgers dripping with melty cheese and a side of crispy fries or, my personal favorite, tater tots, usually with a strawberry shake.

Nobody makes a cheeseburger like they do at truck stops. They remind me of those good old days on the road with some of my favorite people. When I get that craving, I try to go get the real thing, but when that's not possible, this burger hits the spot.

4 potato buns

2 tablespoons salted butter, softened

2 pounds lean ground beef, shaped into 4 patties

Kosher salt, to taste

Freshly ground black pepper, to taste

1 tablespoon Reba's Place Burger Seasoning (p. 121)

8 slices smoked cheddar cheese

¼ cup Reba's Place Remix Sauce (p. 172)

4 large leaves green leaf lettuce

1 heirloom tomato, sliced ½-inch thick

12 slices Reba's Place Bread-and-Butter Pickles (p. 178)

8 slices Reba's Place Brown Sugar Candied Bacon (p. 173)

¼ cup Reba's Place Cherry Coke Barbecue Sauce (p. 176), more to taste

8 Reba's Place Onion and Jalapeño Haystacks (p. 175)

1. Spread the cut sides of each bun evenly with softened butter and set aside.

2. Preheat tbe grill to 450°F.

3. Season the beef patties liberally with salt and pepper. Arrange them on the grill and cook for 9 to 12 minutes, flipping halfway through, until done to your liking. In the last 3 minutes of grilling, season the patties with Reba's Place Burger Seasoning and top each with 2 slices of cheese. While the burgers cook, toast the buns on the other side of the grill.

4. Remove the burgers from the girll. To assemble, spread 1 tablespoon of Reba's Place Remix Sauce onto the bottom half of each bun, then top with a lettuce leaf, tomato slice, and 3 pickles. Place the burger patties on top, followed by 2 slices of Reba's Place Brown Sugar Candied Bacon. Drizzle with Reba's Place Cherry Coke Barbecue Sauce, then top with 2 Reba's Place Onion and Jalapeño Haystacks each. Close the burgers with the top halves of the buns.

Remix Sauce

DIFFICULTY

MAKES ABOUT 1¼ CUPS
PREP TIME: 5 MINUTES

This sauce may look simple, but don't be fooled! Remix Sauce is the perfect accompaniment to so many of my favorite foods—burgers, fries, tots, fried okra, even on a baked potato if you're looking for a comforting kick.

½ cup ketchup

½ cup mayonnaise (I love Duke's)

¼ cup yellow mustard

Kosher salt, to taste

1. Place the ketchup, mayonnaise, mustard, and salt in a mixing bowl and whisk until smooth. Transfer to an airtight container and keep refrigerated for up to 1 week.

Baked Macaroni and Cheese

DIFFICULTY

1 (16-ounce) box large elbow noodles

9 tablespoons salted butter, divided

1/2 cup all-purpose flour

3 cups whole milk

1 cup half and half

1/2 teaspoon ground mustard powder

1/2 teaspoon paprika

1/4 teaspoon garlic powder

Dash of cayenne pepper, more to taste

1/2 teaspoon kosher salt

Freshly ground black pepper, to taste

3 ounces cream cheese, softened

8 ounces Velveeta, cubed

12 ounces sharp cheddar cheese, freshly shredded (about 3 cups)*

36 buttery round crackers, finely crushed (like Ritz)

*Or a mix of sharp cheddar and Gouda, Gruyère, Havarti, or Fontina cheese.

1. Preheat the oven to 350°F. Lightly grease a 4-quart baking dish.

2. Bring a pot of salted water to a boil. Add the noodles, stirring occasionally, until not quite cooked, about 6 minutes. Drain and rinse under cold water. Set aside.

3. Melt 6 tablespoons of the butter over medium heat. Add the flour and whisk it steadily into the butter until the mixture turns golden, about 1 minute.

4. Slowly stream the milk and half and half into the pot while continuing to whisk, dissolving any lumps. Add the mustard, paprika, garlic powder, cayenne, salt, and pepper. Whisk steadily as the sauce heats, until it begins to thicken, about 4 to 5 minutes. Remove the pot from the heat.

5. Drop the cream cheese by the spoonful into the sauce and stir. Add the cubed Velveeta and stir until mostly melted. Add the shredded cheese, stirring slowly after each handful, until the sauce is smooth.

6. Add the noodles to the cheese sauce and fold until coated. Pour the mixture into the baking dish.

7. Place the remaining 3 tablespoons of butter in a large microwave-safe bowl. Microwave on high for about 30 seconds, or until melted. Add the crushed crackers to the bowl and mix until evenly moistened.

8. Sprinkle the cracker crumbs over the macaroni and cheese. Transfer to the middle rack of the oven.

9. Bake for 20 to 23 minutes, until the topping is golden brown. Remove the dish from the oven. Allow to cool for 10 to 15 minutes before serving.

Bread-and-Butter Pickles

MAKES ABOUT 6 CUPS
PREP TIME: 1 HOUR
INACTIVE TIME: 5 DAYS

DIFFICULTY

PICKLES

1 pound cucumbers, sliced 1/4-inch thick

1 1/2 cups kosher salt, divided

5 cups ice cubes

1 yellow onion, thinly sliced

4 large stalks celery, thinly sliced

BRINE

2 cups distilled white vinegar

2 cups apple cider vinegar

1 cup water

1/4 cup kosher salt

1 cup plus 2 tablespoons white sugar

1/2 cup honey

1 tablespoon celery seed

1/2 teaspoon red pepper flakes

1/2 teaspoon mustard seeds

1/2 teaspoon fenugreek seeds

1/2 teaspoon whole cloves

1/2 teaspoon allspice berries

1/2 teaspoon turmeric

I'll admit, these are some fancy pickles. They take longer to make than I'd like (you have to wait five days to eat them!), but good things come to those who wait.

1. Place the cucumber slices in a large bowl. Sprinkle with 1 cup of salt and add 2/3 of the ice cubes. Toss gently to coat.

2. Place the onion and celery in a separate bowl. Sprinkle with the remaining 1/2 cup of salt and add the remaining ice cubes. Toss gently to coat. Let the mixtures rest for 1 hour, stirring both every 10 minutes.

3. Rinse the cucumbers with cold water. Discard any unmelted ice cubes. Do the same for the onions and celery.

4. Layer the rinsed cucumbers with the onion and celery in an 8-quart storage container.

5. Place vinegars, water, salt, sugar, honey, celery, red pepper, mustard, fenugreek, cloves, berries, and turmeric in a large saucepan and set over medium-high heat. Bring to a boil. Once boiling, remove the pan from the heat.

6. Carefully pour the hot brine over the vegetables.

7. Place a square of parchment over the vegetables. Set a plate on top of the parchment, allowing the brine to rise over it as it weighs down the vegetables.

11

Do What You Love

Country music brings people together. It's very relatable, and that's what people like to listen to—something they can relate to. If you sing a sad song, someone in the crowd always goes, "Oh my gosh, she's singing that for me." Country songs are all about telling a good story. They have this special power to bring up memories and feelings from the past, taking you back to your childhood or a special relationship. And they aren't afraid to lean into the tough stuff in life either, but they tackle it in a way that can help people connect. It's such a special genre of music, and I think that's why it has endured for so long.

I'm so blessed to have gotten to be part of country music for so many years, and I love getting to wake up every day and do what I love.

A good sign that you're doing what you love is when you're willing to fight for it. For a really long time, the thought of getting a number one song really drove me. I was willing to work for it, no matter how tough it was or how long it took. I released thirteen singles from five albums before I got a number one. A lot of people don't realize how very unglamorous

Music Brings People Together

The song "Back to God" was a song Randy Houser had on his debut album. I loved it so much.

When it was time to record my gospel album, I decided to give it a shot. It was the first single we released from the album. I immediately added it to my live show. When Brooks & Dunn and I were in Las Vegas, I would look out in the audience and see people with their hands in the air, praising the Lord. In Vegas! I didn't expect that!

I got the chance to sing it with Lauren Daigle for the Academy of Country Music (ACM) awards, and we enjoyed singing it so much that we decided to release a fully produced version together. And if that wasn't enough, we did it again with just the piano as part of my 2018 Christmas album, *My Kind of Christmas*.

Songs like "Back to God" are my favorite type of songs to record and perform over and over because they really touch people. It's amazing how everyone loves to talk about that song. I guess it affects them the same way it has affected me through the years, and that is a beautiful thing.

Recording the Grammy award–winning "Back to God" music video at the Tulip Street United Methodist Church, 2017

It's All in the Listening

Maybe you're trying to make a decision or a change related to your career. If you're trying to get on a new path but feel unsure what your next step should be, the best thing you can do is start listening. Here are a few takeaways for what to do when you're seeking advice.

* **Be still.** The first thing you need to do is turn down the noise in your life. When you get quiet, you can hear the voice of God so much better.

* **Trust that God will show up.** He may not talk so that you hear Him with your ears. Sometimes He answers with a feeling, sometimes with a push in the right direction. I believe that we talk to God in whatever way works best for us, and He answers in the way He knows we'll hear.

* **Find your teachers.** I've found teachers at every stage of my life, whether in a classroom in Oklahoma or a studio in Nashville. I try to listen to anyone who can teach me about business, the industry, music, and just basic things you want to know about life.

* **Trust your team.** Whether this is your family, your network of friends, or some really great coworkers, it's important to have people who know what motivates you. They can be a second gut check when you need one.

The next time you're faced with a decision, go somewhere quiet to think it through. What feelings are bubbling up? Does one path feel a little more right than the other? That might be God trying to tell you something.

Building a life you love, doing what you love, filling that life with people you love—none of that happens by accident. I give God total credit for everything in my life. I give Him credit for helping me find a career that I love. I give Him credit for bringing me the people to help me build a life I love. The only thing I can take credit for is that I listened.

The producers of *Tremors* saw me on *The Pat Sajak Show* and called me in for an audition. When my agent sent the script, I told him I wanted to do the movie before I even finished reading it.

"Did you finish it?"

"No, not yet," I said.

Hanging out with my Tremors onscreen husband, Michael Gross, California, 1989

"Well, finish it and call me back."

But I knew in my gut that this was a great opportunity. It was a movie that really caught my interest and imagination.

The producers liked me, but I don't think they were sold on hiring a singer known for her big stage shows and even bigger hair.

"You're not going to be able to wear makeup," they told me.

"Yeah, that's fine."

"Your hair's going to be up in a pony-tail," they said.

"That's fine."

"Reba, this is gonna be a down-and-dirty desert monster movie."

"Okay, okay, *I got it*," I assured them.

They really wanted me to know that this wasn't going to be a glamorous role. And boy, they weren't kidding. It was rough! The hours were long. It was hot, and dirty, and dusty, and to top it off, I was doing concerts on the weekends and filming the movie during the week. But all of the dust and dirt was worth it because I loved that script and felt honored to be part of such a fun movie.

I knew I wanted to do more acting work, but schedules aren't always easy to

CAKE

1³/4 cups sugar

1¹/4 cups cake flour (sold in the baking aisle near the all-purpose flour)

¹/4 teaspoon salt

12 egg whites, room temperature

1¹/2 teaspoons cream of tartar

1 teaspoon vanilla extract

1 tablespoon Grand Marnier (optional)

CAKE

1. Preheat the oven to 350°F. Have ready a 9-inch tube pan. Do not grease.

2. Place the sugar in the bowl of a food processor. Pulse until very fine and powdery. Remove 1 cup of the sugar and set aside. Add the flour and salt to the food processor and pulse a few times to aerate.

3. Place the egg whites and cream of tartar in a very clean, completely dry mixing bowl. Beat with a hand mixer on medium-high speed until foamy, about 2 minutes. With the mixer running, slowly add the reserved 1 cup of sugar to the bowl. Continue beating until the egg whites double in volume and begin to hold soft peaks. Add the vanilla and Grand Marnier (if using), and beat until the mixture holds medium peaks.

4. Sift the flour mixture into the egg whites in three additions, folding with a very light hand after each, until the batter is just combined.

5. Gently pour the batter into the tube pan and spread it into an even layer. Transfer to the lower-middle rack of the oven.

6. Bake for 40 to 45 minutes, or until a toothpick inserted in the center of the cake comes out clean. (Do not open the oven while the cake is baking, or it will deflate!)

7. Remove the pan from the oven. Turn the cake upside down onto a wire rack without removing the pan. Cool for at least 2 hours. Once cool, run a knife between the edges of the cake and the pan, then tap the bottom until the cake releases.

8. To serve, slice the cake into generous portions and arrange on serving plates. Spoon ¹/4 cup of strawberries with their juices onto the cake, and top with a big dollop of the whipped cream.

Pineapple Mojito with Pineapple-Infused Rum

MAKES 1 DRINK
PREP TIME: 10 MINUTES
INACTIVE TIME: 3 DAYS OR MORE

DIFFICULTY

PINEAPPLE-INFUSED RUM

1 ripe pineapple, crown and rind removed

1 vanilla bean, split in half lengthwise

1/2-inch piece fresh ginger root, peeled and sliced

750 milliliters silver rum (like Flor de Caña Blanco Four-Year Rum)

PINEAPPLE MOJITO

6 to 8 leaves fresh mint

1 slice lime, plus more for garnish

2 ounces Reba's Place Pineapple-Infused Rum

1/2 ounce fresh lime juice

1/2 ounce simple syrup

1 (7.5-ounce) mini can ginger ale

1 wedge rum-infused pineapple, for garnish

1 sprig fresh mint leaves, for garnish

If you're looking for a way to make your movie night a little more fun, try making a couple of these! You don't have to make your own pineapple-infused rum for these mojitos, but if you're feeling fancy, give it a try!

PINEAPPLE-INFUSED RUM

MAKES ABOUT 4 CUPS

1. Core the pineapple and slice into 1/2-inch thick rings. Cut each ring into 3 wedges and stack them neatly in a large, wide-mouthed glass jar. Add the vanilla bean and ginger.

2. Pour the rum into the jar, fully covering the fruit.

3. Secure a lid on the jar and place it in a cool, dark place. Allow it to infuse for at least 3 days, but preferably 1 week, before using.

PINEAPPLE MOJITO

1. Place the mint leaves and lime slice in a tall glass and muddle together. Fill the glass with ice.

2. Pour the Pineapple-Infused Rum, lime juice, and simple syrup into the glass and stir to combine. Top with ginger ale.

3. Garnish the drink with a pineapple wedge left over from the Pineapple-Infused Rum, a sprig of mint, and a slice of lime. Enjoy!

basketball and rodeos. Mama never had anyone to encourage her to follow her dreams. She pushed me because she wanted to do for me what no one had done for her.

Mama was always my biggest cheerleader. She traveled with me, helped me work on my songs, and was there for me every step of the way when I needed advice and support. When my singles didn't go up the charts the way we wanted them to or I got passed over for opportunities, she gave me the pep talks I needed. The first year we went to Fan Fair, I sat at the PolyGram/Mercury booth, waiting for a fan to come by and ask for my autograph. One couple walked up to the booth, looked at my name, and then looked at me. Mama said, "Reba, get your pen ready!" But instead they asked me if I knew where the bathroom was. I just put my pen down and said, "Yeah, it's right around the corner." Mama and I just smiled at each other—what else could we do? There's a reason I accepted my first CMA Female Vocalist of the Year award in my mama's honor. I don't know where I'd be without her.

Alice was another early role model for me. As my older sister, she went through everything first. And she understood what it was like at school and competing in the rodeo as a girl in a way that Daddy and Pake did not. We all looked up to Alice because she took care of us. She watched out for us. She would fight a chainsaw for us. She tried to teach me how

to be fierce and to fight for the things that mattered to me. And she has kept teaching me that my whole life.

When Alice had her youngest daughter, Haley, there were some serious complications. The doctors said Haley would probably never make it out of the hospital. But she did, and she's thriving today, and I credit God, Alice, and Robert (Alice's husband and Haley's daddy) for that. Alice's faith in God shines through in everything she does, especially when it comes to being Haley's mama. Alice and Robert both love the Lord, and I think God gave Haley to them because they have tons of faith and love for Haley.

Haley is the result of what love can do. Haley lives with severe physical and developmental disabilities, but she is deeply loved by us and by God. I know life doesn't look anything like Alice had imagined when she first discovered she was pregnant. But Haley has taught us all so much about unconditional love and accepting others as they are, and she's brought

Shelby helped me stay in the moment, and I always wanted to make sure I put him first. I worked a lot back when Shelby was little, but my desire to be near him changed the whole way I operated. It started even before he was born. By the end of 1989, when I was pregnant with him, we started flying from concert to concert because I thought the bus rides were too rough on the baby. Just after the last show of the year, when I was five months pregnant, my doctor put me on bedrest in the hospital for most of December and January. It forced me to slow down and focus on him, and that's something I'll never regret. I would have hung by my toenails to have that child.

When he was a baby and toddler, we took him everywhere with us. Once he started school and couldn't tour with us, we started flying home late at night after every show just to make sure we could wake up with Shelby. I would take him to school, pick him up from school, and be there with him until it was time to fly back out to the next show and do it all again. It was worth the hours in the air to gain the hours with him during the day.

Shelby helped me remember how fun it is to be goofy and silly. He brought out the kid in me. I was always happy to get down on the floor and play with him, and no one in the world makes me laugh like Shelby. Being his mom pushed me outside my comfort zone in good ways. For instance, I'd had a fear of ice ever since I was a little kid when I watched our frozen pond crack under Susie's feet. So of course, Shelby fell head over heels for ice hockey and played for years, which meant I found myself going to as many games as I could to cheer him on. I also don't think I'd seen a race until Shelby decided to become a race car driver. Now I've learned quite a bit about the world of racing. Kids have a way of pushing you out of your comfort zone.

Shelby has entered a new phase in his life and has brought a new member into our family. Marissa and Shelby were married February 12, 2022. We love her with all our hearts! I'm so happy she is my daughter-in-law.

Finding a good mentor is important, and it doesn't have to be complicated. Look around for someone a little further down the path, or maybe even a child in your life. Talk to them, ask questions, and just get to know them a little. Most mentoring happens in the small moments with a piece of offhand advice here or there. There's something to learn from every person you meet if you're willing to look for it.

Mama's Pimento Cheese Sandwich

MAKES 1 SANDWICH
PREP TIME: 20 MINUTES
INACTIVE TIME: 1 HOUR

DIFFICULTY

It would tickle Mama to know that she inspired a sandwich in my restaurant. I love that her tradition lives on. And with fresh-made pimento cheese, it's even more special. At the restaurant, we prefer to grate blocks of cheese to avoid the additives used to prevent clumping in pre-shredded cheese. For this recipe, it's especially important.

PIMENTO CHEESE

4 ounces cream cheese, softened (1/2 bar)

1/2 cup mayonnaise (I love Duke's)

1 tablespoon Dijon mustard

1 teaspoon Worcestershire sauce

1 teaspoon hot sauce (like Crystal)

1 teaspoon paprika

1/2 teaspoon granulated garlic

1/2 teaspoon granulated onion

1 cup sharp Cheddar cheese, shredded (about 4 ounces)

1 cup pepper jack cheese, shredded (about 4 ounces)

1 (4-ounce) jar diced pimento peppers, drained

Kosher salt, to taste

Freshly ground black pepper, to taste

PIMENTO CHEESE SANDWICH

2 tablespoons salted butter, softened

2 slices sourdough bread

1 tablespoon Miracle Whip

1/2 cup Reba's Place Pimento Cheese

2 thick slices heirloom or beefsteak tomato

PIMENTO CHEESE

MAKES ABOUT 3 CUPS OF CHEESE FOR 6 SANDWICHES

1. Place the cream cheese, mayonnaise, Dijon, Worcestershire, hot sauce, paprika, garlic, and onion in a large mixing bowl. Beat with a hand mixer on medium speed until smooth and creamy, about 3 minutes.

2. Fold in the shredded cheeses and pimentos with a rubber spatula until combined. Add salt and pepper to taste.

3. Cover the bowl with plastic wrap and refrigerate for at least 1 hour before serving. Keep refrigerated in an airtight container for up to 1 week.

PIMENTO CHEESE SANDWICH

1. Set a skillet or griddle over medium heat. Spread the butter onto one side of each slice of bread.

Meatloaf

DIFFICULTY ⚬—⚬ ⚬—⚬ ⚬—⚬

At Reba's Place, we grind our locally sourced meat from our partners at the Choctaw Nation fresh each day. You can ask your butcher to grind it for you or use already-ground pork and beef. You can make this as fancy as you choose!

1 cup old-fashioned oats (not quick-cooking oats)

2 pounds lean ground beef

1 pound ground pork

1 cup panko breadcrumbs

¼ cup heavy cream

2 slices white or sourdough bread, crusts removed

2 cups cremini mushrooms, halved (8 ounces)

1 yellow onion, roughly chopped

2 stalks celery, roughly chopped

1 large carrot, peeled and roughly chopped

¼ cup (½ stick) salted butter

4 cloves garlic, minced

2 tablespoons tomato paste

2 eggs

1 small handful fresh parsley, finely chopped

1 tablespoon Worcestershire sauce

1 teaspoon hot sauce

1½ teaspoons kosher salt, plus more to taste

1½ teaspoons seasoned salt (like Lawry's)

½ teaspoon freshly ground black pepper

½ cup Reba's Place Tangy Barbecue Sauce (p. 217)

1. Preheat the oven to 350°F. Spray a 9 x 5-inch loaf pan with nonstick cooking spray.

2. Spread the oats onto a baking sheet in an even layer. Transfer to the middle rack of the oven. Toast until fragrant, about 12 to 15 minutes.

3. While the oats toast, place the ground pork and beef in a large mixing bowl. Sprinkle evenly with the panko breadcrumbs, then pour in the heavy cream. Cover the bowl with plastic wrap and transfer to the refrigerator.

4. Remove the baking sheet from the oven. Increase the temperature to 375°F.

5. Transfer the oats to the bowl of a food processor along with the sliced bread. Pulse until very fine. Sprinkle the crumbs over the meat and cream mixture, then return the bowl to the refrigerator.

6. Place the mushrooms, onions, celery, and carrot in the bowl of the food processor. Pulse until finely chopped, to roughly the same size as the ground meat.

7. Melt the butter in a large skillet over medium-high heat. Add the vegetables and sauté until softened and lightly browned, about 6 to 7 minutes. Add the garlic and tomato paste. Cook for an additional 2 minutes, stirring to coat the vegetables. Remove the skillet from the heat and allow the vegetables to cool.

8. Add eggs, parsley, Worcestershire, hot sauce, salts, and pepper to the meat mixture. Begin to mix gently with gloved hands or a large wooden spoon. Add the cooled vegetables and continue mixing until all the ingredients are just combined.

9. Press the meat mixture firmly into the loaf pan, ensuring there are no air pockets. Invert the loaf onto a parchment-lined baking sheet and carefully lift off the pan. Gently round and smooth the edges of the loaf with clean, damp hands. Transfer to the middle rack of the oven.

10. Bake for 45 minutes, or until the meatloaf reaches an internal temperature of 155°F. Brush the top of the loaf with Reba's Place Tangy Barbecue Sauce. Continue baking for 15 to 20 minutes, until the sauce is slightly caramelized.

11. Remove the baking sheet from the oven. Allow the meatloaf to rest for at least 10 minutes before slicing and serving.

Like It Fancy?

At Reba's Place, we serve this meatloaf as an open-faced sandwich on our home-made sourdough bread with Reba's Place Onion and Jalapeño Haystacks (p. 175), but it's also great with Baked Macaroni and Cheese (p. 177) and green beans or mashed potatoes and mushroom gravy!

9. Remove the skillet from the oven. Allow the cake to rest for 15 minutes—no more, no less, or the topping will stick!

10. Hold a serving plate facedown over the skillet, then swiftly flip the skillet to invert the cake on the plate. Allow the cake to cool completely before serving.

Hanging with my kids Shelby, Chassidy, Brandon, and Shawna

Let them fail. Letting them win all the time or stepping in to save the day won't do them any favors. You can ask Shelby—I never let him win at games. Our housekeeper at the time, Rose, used to get so aggravated with me about that, but I knew he'd learn more from losing honestly than if I let him win every time. Life is tough; kids need to be able to be tough too. But let them still be soft with you when they need it. Hold them accountable for their actions. If they say they'll do something, make sure they do it. Don't let little lies and half-truths slip by. Most importantly, make sure they know that they are loved and valued. That's the legacy that will last the longest in your own family and, hopefully, encourage the next generation to be a little better and wiser than those of us who came before.

Christmas Traditions

When I was a kid, Pake, Alice, Susie, and I would wake up and run down the hall in our pajamas (or in Pake's case, his underwear) as soon as we woke up on Christmas morning to open our presents. It was pure chaos as we all ripped open our gifts at once. There was no taking turns or pausing to admire things. We were like wild animals! And every year, Mama would make banana pudding to leave out for Santa Claus. That just so happened to be Daddy's favorite dessert too!

When Shelby and Chelsea were younger, our traditions included decorating Christmas trees as a family, setting cookies out for Santa, and then getting up early to open presents. We loved watching *Christmas Vacation* every Christmas Eve, opening presents, and eating a special Christmas dinner with the family. Then we'd head out for a ski vacation the day after Christmas.

Times have changed, and so have our traditions. Sometimes I get to see Shelby on Christmas and sometimes I don't. When I do see Shelby and Marissa, at Christmas, we still love our holiday

Left: A young Alice and me unwrapping gifts together Christmas morning, Eastern Oklahoma, 1958

Right: Looking at Christmas lights around town with Rex, Marissa, and Shelby, Nashville, Tennessee, 2022

Redhead 'Rita

DIFFICULTY

'RITA

1½ ounces tequila blanco

½ ounce Solerno Blood
Orange Liqueur

½ ounce Ancho Reyes
Chile Liqueur

1 ounce prickly pear
puree (or guava or
watermelon juice)

1 ounce fresh
raspberry puree

1 ounce fresh lime juice

½ ounce agave syrup
(or simple syrup)

5 drops saltwater
(or a dash of salt)

1 slice lime, for garnish

RIM

¼ cup Himalayan pink salt

¼ cup freeze-dried
raspberries, blended
into powder

1 tablespoon sweetened
lime juice

Around here we like to call it a marga-Reba.

1. Fill a margarita glass with ice and set aside to chill.

2. Fill a cocktail shaker with ice. Add in the tequila, liqueurs, purees, lime juice, syrup, and saltwater and shake vigorously to combine.

3. Whisk together the salt and raspberries in a small bowl. Pour into a shallow dish. Place the sweetened lime juice into a separate shallow dish.

4. Discard the ice from the margarita glass. Dip the glass in sweetened lime juice, then into the salt mixture, pressing firmly to create a thick rim. Fill the glass just below the rim with fresh ice.

5. Strain the drink into the center of the glass. Garnish with a slice of lime, and enjoy!

Keep Dreaming Forward

I once asked Daddy after I had won an award, "Daddy, when you won the steer roping world championship, what was more fun? Winning the big belt buckle and the saddle? Or the getting there?" He didn't hesitate. He said, "The getting there." And that's how I feel too. The awards and accolades I've received are the best, but they've never been nearly as much fun as the getting there.

I always like to have something to look forward to—a new kind of project, a place to visit, or a new album. But for me, it's not about the end result as much as it is about all the fun and hard work you experience along the way. During the early days of the pandemic, having time off from constant touring helped me find a new level of balance between work and play. It also gave me time to think through all that I've gotten to do, figure out what I'd like to do again, and maybe even find some new things to try!

Wisdom from the Greats

I will forever be grateful for the women who came before me in country music. Dolly Parton, Bobbie Gentry, Loretta Lynn, Tammy Wynette, Kitty Wells, Skeeter Davis, Wanda Jackson, Jeannie C. Riley, Norma Jean Beasler, Connie Smith, Barbara Mandrell, Anne Murray, Dottie West, Emmylou Harris, June Carter Cash, and Brenda Lee blazed a trail for the rest of us to follow.

I've been lucky enough to get to work with many of my heroes. I didn't always want to meet them because I was afraid they wouldn't turn out to be as nice as I'd imagined, but that isn't how things have turned out at all. These absolute legends were every bit as warm, welcoming, and kind as you could possibly imagine, and they have given me so much inspiration, advice, and friendship. Here are some of the things I've learned from these special women:

---

* **Work hard.** There is no substitute for putting in the time and effort.

* **Be honest.** Your reputation is worth its weight in gold, and having integrity will get you further than you might think.

* **Show up on time.** No one wants to work with someone who isn't respectful of others' time.

* **Be prepared.** If you're professional and ready to go, others will be too.

* **Be different.** Stand out for being yourself.

* **Appreciate your team.** Treat everyone equally, with kindness and respect. Just like Dolly does.

On set with Dolly Parton filming our cover of "Does He Love You," Nashville, Tennessee, 2021

I love to work with artists I admire. When we were putting together my *Revived Remixed Revisited* box set, I knew I wanted to rerecord my 1993 Grammy award–winning song "Does He Love You" that I sang with Linda Davis. I wanted to find the perfect voice to make it feel fresh. We had so many names on the list, but my first choice was Dolly Parton. Dolly and I have been friends for more than thirty years, but we've never recorded a duet together. The song is such a fan favorite, and it fit her voice perfectly. It was a dream come true for me, and we ended up receiving a Grammy nomination for Best Country Duo/Group Performance. The fact that I could be nominated again for the same song thirty years later with Dolly was simply the best!

I've been lucky to work with some of the best in the business over the course of my music career, and I've learned so much from them. Country music has changed a lot since the 1970s when I was just starting out, and it's never been as diverse as it is right now. I love meeting the new artists who are helping shape the future of the genre I love so much.

I always try to stay open to new ideas and opportunities that come my way, but when my team suggested I consider making a podcast, I was hesitant. I hadn't listened to many podcasts, and I had no idea what I would talk about. It took us some trial and error to figure out what we were doing. We tweaked as we went along, and we ended up with something really cool that I have enjoyed doing. Melissa Peterman and I had a wonderful time during the first season. I did the second season by myself. I sure did learn a lot, and I had a lot of fun doing it. You can listen to both seasons on Spotify.

———

My career as an actor continues to challenge me as well. I've enjoyed getting to play some characters that are unlike any I've ever played before. In the fall of 2022 and early 2023, I got to play Sunny Barnes on the third season of ABC's hit series *Big Sky*. It was fun to see my fans' reactions to the idea of me possibly being a villain. And I loved getting to act alongside Rex, who played my husband, Buck Barnes! I also had the opportunity to play Judge Kim Wheeler in Lifetime's *The Hammer*, which was based on the real-life story of traveling judge Kim Wanker. The best part was that Rex and Melissa Peterman were in it too. Both of these character roles stretched me as an actor, and I had a blast trying something new.

———

Opening our restaurant, Reba's Place, was incredibly special for me and unlike anything I'd ever done before. Carol Ervin, a great friend of the family, was working on reinvigorating the downtown of Atoka, Oklahoma, which is between Tulsa and Dallas on Highway 69/75. She was looking for partners who would bring businesses and tourists to their Main Street, and she called to see if I'd be interested in being part of starting a restaurant. I said, "Are you on crack?!"

My Guide to Nashville

When I moved here in the 1980s, people would describe Nashville as "a small town disguised as a big city." Not anymore! It's diversifying and attracting new businesses, all while holding on to its original charm. Here's my guide to celebrating some of the classic and more current spots around town.

	CLASSIC	CURRENT
BREAKFAST	Founded in 1961, **The Pancake Pantry** is one of the most popular spots here in town. Little known fact—we filmed the opening shots of the "Is There Life Out There" music video here.	If you're looking for a classic Southern brunch, head over to **Biscuit Love**, a locally owned family business serving up some of the best biscuits and gravy you can imagine.
LUNCH	**Midtown Cafe** has been a local mainstay for over three decades, and I hope it's here to stay for many decades to come. Get the meatloaf—it's my favorite.	After twenty years of service, **Green Hills Grille** closed its doors in 2008. When it reopened in 2015 in its new location, all of us locals were very happy. They serve the best Mediterranean salad in town.
LIVE MUSIC	Decade after decade, **The Bluebird Cafe** keeps churning out some of the top names in country. The acoustic "In the Round" shows are some of my favorites, when songwriters sit around in a circle and share the stories behind their songs.	**The Listening Room Cafe** also has a great lineup of up-and-coming singer-songwriters, and you never know—you might be one of the first to hear the next big hit in country music.
DINNER	If you want to get fancy for a night out, head over to **Valentino's Ristorante**. They serve Italian food—can't go wrong!	**Bourbon Steak** by Michael Mina also cooks up a mean steak with a little-bit-fancy atmosphere.

Mama's books on display from floor to ceiling at my restaurant, Reba's Place, Atoka, Oklahoma, 2023

Southeastern Oklahoma will always be home to me, and it felt like a great opportunity for the city of Atoka. Carol was excited about the idea, but it really came together when we found the right partner, the Choctaw Nation. I've often performed at their casinos and have a wonderful relationship with them. Chef Kurtess agreed to help get it going. Once they were on board, the development of the restaurant picked up steam.

I loved getting the chance to weigh in to make sure it has personal touches that make the place feel like me. Alice, Susie, and I asked for a section of the upstairs to be made into a library filled with the books Mama left behind when she passed. It has been such a fun time getting to work with Chef Kurtess Mortensen, manager Garett Smith, all the staff, all the folks in Atoka, and the wonderful team from the Choctaw Nation. The team who brought Reba's Place to life is so creative, and I'm very blessed to have this opportunity and to hopefully leave a legacy in the community where I grew up.

Lately I've been dreaming about what else may be in the future. Maybe someday, I'd like to revisit Broadway in another show, preferably one with a strong female ensemble cast, maybe something like *Steel Magnolias*. I've also thought about doing a smaller theater tour that could be a mix of storytelling and music. I never know what's coming next, but I'm always listening for God to let me in on the next right thing.

I also want to travel more. I've been all over the world on tour, but that didn't always mean I got to see those places the way I wanted to. Having the chance to travel with Rex, my family, and my friends is something I plan to keep making more time for. Some of my most cherished memories are trips I took with my family, especially ones with Mama and Daddy. I want to make sure I keep making a life of memories.

And of course, the one thing I know for sure is that country music will always be part of who I am and what I do. I'm lucky enough to collaborate with the best musicians and greatest songwriters Nashville has to offer and record songs that connect with my fans, and that is something I will never take for granted. Music will always be my first love. Even as I try new things and go on other adventures, everything always comes back to the music, and I'm looking forward to being back in a studio recording more new songs soon. The year 2025 will be my fiftieth anniversary in the music business. I can't wait to see what's in store for us!

For every dream I have, I keep asking God for guidance. It's sort of like Garth Brooks's song "Unanswered Prayers." God may not give me the things I want on *my* timeline, but if it's His will, it will be His will, His way, in His time. Whether or not I get what I desire, He wants us to keep asking, so I do. And I can't wait to see what He says yes to for me next!

Fried Avocado Slices

MAKES 4 SERVINGS
PREP TIME: 25 MINUTES
COOK TIME: 15 MINUTES

DIFFICULTY

CREMA

1/2 cup Mexican crema (or sour cream), for serving

1 tablespoon fresh lime juice

1 1/2 teaspoons hot sauce, more or less to taste (try a Serrano pepper hot sauce)

Kosher salt, to taste

AVOCADOS

1 quart peanut oil (or vegetable oil), for frying

2 large avocados, peeled, pitted, and sliced 1/2-inch thick

3/4 teaspoon kosher salt, divided

1 tablespoon fresh lime juice

1/2 cup all-purpose flour

1/2 teaspoon freshly ground black pepper, divided

2 egg whites

1 tablespoon water

1 cup panko breadcrumbs

1 cup plain breadcrumbs

1 cup grated Parmesan cheese

1 teaspoon seasoned salt (like Lawry's)

1/2 teaspoon granulated garlic

1/2 teaspoon granulated onion

1 small handful fresh cilantro, finely chopped, for garnish

1/2 cup salsa verde, for serving

If you're looking for a new way to serve up an avocado, try frying it! Once you start eating them, you won't want to stop. They are great as a side for burgers or tacos.

1. Place the crema, lime juice, hot sauce, and a large pinch of salt in a small mixing bowl and whisk to combine. Cover the bowl with plastic wrap and refrigerate until ready to use.

2. Attach a thermometer to the side of a large Dutch oven and add the peanut oil. Heat the oil to 350°F and maintain the temperature within a range of 25°F.

3. Line a baking sheet with parchment paper. Set a cooling rack on top of a second baking sheet and place it next to the Dutch oven.

4. While the oil heats, place the avocado slices on a plate. Sprinkle with 1/4 teaspoon of salt and the lime juice. Set aside.

5. Place the flour, remaining 1/2 teaspoon of salt, and 1/4 teaspoon of pepper in a shallow bowl. Whisk to combine. In a second bowl, whisk together the

egg whites and water until lightly frothy. Place the panko, breadcrumbs, Parmesan, seasoned salt, garlic, onion, and remaining $1/4$ teaspoon of pepper in a third shallow bowl. Whisk to combine.

6. Gently toss the avocado slices in the flour mixture until evenly coated. Transfer $1/3$ of the slices into the egg whites and stir to coat. Lift the slices from the bowl using a large fork and transfer them to the panko mixture. Turn the slices with the fork until evenly coated, then carefully transfer them to the baking sheet. Repeat with the remaining avocado slices.

7. Fry the avocado slices in 3 to 4 batches until deeply golden brown, about 4 minutes. Carefully lift them from the oil using a deep fryer skimmer and transfer to the cooling rack.

8. Arrange the fried avocado slices on a plate and drizzle with crema. Sprinkle with chopped fresh cilantro. Serve with a side of salsa verde.

NOLA Shrimp and Grits

DIFFICULTY

If you're looking for a fun way to reinvent this New Orleans classic, try this version featuring blue corn grits. These grits deliver a beautiful purple hue that makes this dish look like a million bucks.

GRITS

1 cup blue corn grits (or yellow grits)

2 cups water

2 cups low-sodium chicken stock

1/2 cup (1 stick) unsalted butter, cubed

1/2 teaspoon kosher salt, plus more to taste

Freshly ground black pepper, to taste

SHRIMP

1 tablespoon olive oil

4 cloves garlic, finely chopped

1 sprig fresh rosemary

Zest of 1/2 lemon

1 tablespoon sweet paprika

1 tablespoon Cajun seasoning, divided

1 tablespoon tomato paste

1 cup beer (preferably lager)

1 cup low-sodium shrimp stock (or chicken stock)

Juice of 1/2 lemon

1 tablespoon Worcestershire sauce

1 teaspoon hot sauce

1/2 cup all-purpose flour

11/2 pounds large raw shrimp, peeled and deveined

1/2 cup unsalted butter, divided

1/2 cup diced tasso ham (about 4 ounces)

4 green onions, finely chopped, divided

GRITS

1. Place the grits in a fine-mesh sieve and rinse with cool water.

2. Place the grits and water in a large pot and set over medium heat. Bring to a simmer, stirring frequently.

3. Pour the chicken stock into a separate saucepan and bring to a simmer over medium heat.

4. Add a couple ladles of chicken stock to the simmering grits and stir. Simmer for about 10 minutes, until the stock is mostly absorbed, then add a couple more ladles. Repeat until all the stock has been added to the grits.

5. Once the grits are very soft, turn the heat to as low as it goes. Add the butter and salt. Stir gently until the butter is fully melted into the grits. Add additional salt and pepper to taste. Keep warm while you prepare the shrimp.

SHRIMP

1. Add the olive oil to a large saucepan and set it over medium heat. Add the garlic, rosemary sprig, lemon zest, paprika, $1^{1}/_{2}$ teaspoons of Cajun seasoning, and tomato paste. Sauté just until fragrant, about 1 minute.

2. Pour the beer into the pan, scraping up any browned bits from the bottom. Add the stock, lemon juice, Worcestershire, and hot sauce, and stir to combine. Simmer the liquid until it is reduced by half, about 10 to 15 minutes.

3. Once reduced, remove the pan from the heat. Discard the rosemary sprig and set aside.

4. In a medium bowl, whisk together the flour and remaining $1^{1}/_{2}$ teaspoons of Cajun seasoning. Add the shrimp to the bowl and toss to coat.

5. Melt 1 tablespoon of butter in a large sauté pan over medium-high heat. Add the tasso ham and cook until browned and crispy, about 5 to 7 minutes. Add the floured shrimp and half the green onions. Cook, stirring constantly, until the shrimp begins to turn pink, about 2 minutes.

6. Pour the reduced stock into the pan and bring to a simmer. Cook until the shrimp are cooked through, about 4 minutes. Turn off the heat. Add the remaining butter to the pan in 3 additions, whisking after each, to form a sauce.

7. Serve the shrimp over bowls of blue corn grits, garnished with the remaining green onion.

Atoka Float

DIFFICULTY

VANILLA SIMPLE SYRUP

1 vanilla bean, split

1 cup sugar

1 cup water

FLOAT

1 1/2 ounces Ole Smoky Banana Pudding Cream Moonshine

1 ounce heavy whipping cream

1/2 ounce Reba's Place Vanilla Simple Syrup

1 (12-ounce) bottle hard root beer (like Not Your Father's root beer)

At Reba's Place, this take-you-back drink is served with a freshly baked chocolate chip cookie.

VANILLA SIMPLE SYRUP

MAKES ABOUT 1½ CUPS

1. Place vanilla bean, sugar, and water in a small saucepan and set over medium-high heat. Bring to a boil.

2. Once boiling, turn the heat to medium-low. Simmer the liquid for 2 minutes, until fragrant. Remove the saucepan from the heat.

3. Remove the vanilla bean and discard. Pour the syrup into a heatproof glass container and refrigerate for at least 12 hours, until chilled. Keep refrigerated in an airtight container for up to 2 months.

FLOAT

1. Place an 18-ounce mug in the freezer for a few hours or overnight.

2. Fill a cocktail shaker with ice. Add the moonshine, cream, and Reba's Place Vanilla Simple Syrup. Shake vigorously to combine.

3. Strain the drink into the frosty mug. Slowly pour the root beer into the glass, letting the froth rise above the top. Enjoy!

15

Here's Your One Chance

As I've mentioned, risk is part of being a McEntire. Rodeo is risky. Life on a ranch is risky. Launching a singing career is risky. Driving race cars is risky. But I'd take a risk any day over playing it safe and missing out. I'm pretty sure Grandpap and Daddy would say the same thing.

Fear is normal, but I also know that if you really want something, you can push past fear to get where you want to go. When I was rodeoing, I saw lots of riders go flying, horses fall, and in some cases, pretty serious injuries in the arena. It's a wonder I had the nerve to get up on that horse and compete after all I'd seen. I'd been watching Alice compete for years before it was my turn, so I knew exactly how dangerous it was. But I knew I wanted to do it. So I practiced and practiced, and I was good in the practice pen. But before each competition, I was still nervous. And yet, I went out and gave it my all every time. I was never as good in a competition as

Promotional shot
in costume as
Colonel Sanders
for my KFC
commercial,
2018

I was in the practice pen, but it wasn't how good I was that mattered in the end. What mattered was that I was willing to take a risk and try my best. I wasn't the best cowgirl out there by any stretch of the imagination, but I learned how to compete even when I was scared.

These days, what scares me more than taking a risk is *not* taking one.

It was a risk to appear as the first-ever female "Colonel Sanders" for Kentucky Fried Chicken (KFC). When KFC approached me, I wasn't sure about it. I didn't know if my fans would like it. I asked just about everyone around me if I should do it. Some people said yes and some said no, but when Aaron Spalding said it would be really cool, I went with that and my gut and signed on. They even agreed to add fringe to Colonel Sanders's famous white suit just for me! The scripts were funny, and it looked like a heckuva lot of fun, so I said yes. I'm so glad I did—it was a hoot!

I had similar thoughts when I was asked to make a cameo in the movie

On set as Trish
in Barb and
Star Go to
Vista Del Mar,
Mexico, 2019

Barb and Star Go to Vista Del Mar. The script was so funny that I laughed out loud reading it, but it was also pretty different from the other movies I'd done. (But then again, *Tremors* had been outside of my wheelhouse too. Who would have expected a country singer to appear in a movie about giant underground killer worms in the desert?) So I took the risk, and I loved it. I got to wear a glamorous dress and film in the water in Cancun. Kristen Wiig and Annie Mumolo were so much fun to work with, and I just about laughed my butt off when I saw the final cut. They didn't advertise my appearance in promos for the film because they really wanted it to be a surprise. That was a risk that paid off too. Most of my fans were thrilled when I popped up!

If you want to stay in any business for a long period of time, you have to keep reinventing yourself. Each risk is also a wonderful opportunity to try something new, to stretch myself, and find new ways to perform. When I recorded "She Thinks His Name Was John," I knew there was the possibility that it could cause some controversy. The song spoke to the AIDS crisis affecting so many people at the time, including people in the industry, musicians, and of course, our fans and the people they loved. I felt like if I could sing about AIDS, people might talk about it more. It's almost like if you shine some light on things in the darkness, they're not so scary. I put any critics out of my mind, and I couldn't have been prouder to have sung that song.

Performing "She Thinks His Name Was John" in front of a replica of the world-famous AIDS Memorial Quilt, 1995

Of course, I've recorded other songs that were risky too. When I wanted to record a song made famous by Bobbie Gentry, I got some push-back. That song is "Fancy," and I've loved it from the moment I heard it back in 1968. My producer at the time, Jimmy Bowen, vetoed the song because it was not good for my image, and he felt it was the wrong choice

REBA #1
CMA AWARDS

REBA #2
CMA AWARDS

REBA #3
CMA AWARDS

Renderings of CMA award costumes by Matt Logan, 2019

for me. I let it go, but I hadn't actually given up on the idea. I was just waiting for the right moment. So when Tony Brown became my producer in 1990, I brought it back up. His immediate response was, "That's my favorite song!" We recorded it for *Rumor Has It* in 1990. It wasn't a number one hit, but I do think it's been the single biggest song of my career. It's the one that everyone knows, even if they aren't a die-hard fan. It's the one I get the most requests for, and it's the song I always end each show with.

In 2019, I was asked to host and perform at the CMA Awards, and they requested that I perform "Fancy" because the research showed people wanted to hear songs they know. Justin McIntosh from my team came to me with an idea to try something totally different. We worked with a new stylist, Matt Logan, for my costumes, and we choreographed a performance with three on-stage costume changes, ending in a pantsuit. We were all so nervous, praying that everything would go off without a hitch (quick costume changes don't always work). It all came together flawlessly, and we were thrilled!

When I perform "Fancy," I always end with my arms wide open, and that's how I want to live my life, wide open and ready to grab what's next, all the laughter and silliness, the love and trust, the friendship and connection—all the good stuff God is bringing to me every day.

After all, the secret to a good life is really not that fancy. What you may see from me on a red carpet or at a concert is only one part of who I am. When the show is over and the lights are turned off, I'm still that girl from Oklahoma who can't wait to get home, kick off my boots, and sit on my porch.

And that's what I hope you take away from this book. Life doesn't have to be fancy. It's the simple moments with loved ones, the inside jokes, dinners on paper plates, and late-night trips to Sonic for a corn dog or a footlong cheese coney and tater tots that make life worth living. It's spending time with family, singing with just a guitar or piano, and having talks with God that keep me grounded. Keep it simple—that will never let you down.

Belting out my signature closing song, "Fancy," at the CMA Awards, Nashville, Tennessee, 2019

Pinto Beans and Cornbread

DIFFICULTY

MAKES 6 SERVINGS
PREP TIME: 40 MINUTES
COOK TIME: 2 HOURS
INACTIVE TIME: 12 HOURS

This is hands-down my favorite food! I've loved pinto beans and cornbread forever! And I still love them. This is the "fancy" version we make at the restaurant, but you don't need a fancy occasion to enjoy them.

PINTO BEANS

1 pound dry pinto beans (about 2 cups)

1 tablespoon kosher salt, plus more to taste

1 (4-ounce) end piece bacon slab, roughly chopped (or 6 slices thick-cut bacon, roughly chopped)

1 yellow onion, whole, peeled

1 carrot, whole, peeled

4 bay leaves

8 cups light chicken stock

1 tablespoon sherry vinegar

Freshly ground black pepper, to taste

Hot sauce, for serving (optional)

CORNBREAD

1½ cups fine cornmeal

½ cup all-purpose flour

1 teaspoon baking powder

½ teaspoon baking soda

1 teaspoon kosher salt

2 large eggs

¼ cup honey

½ cup unsalted butter, melted

1 cup buttermilk (or 1 cup whole milk whisked with 1 teaspoon vinegar)

PINTO BEANS

1. Rinse the beans thoroughly with cold water, then transfer to a large bowl. Fill the bowl with enough fresh water to cover the beans by a few inches. Stir. Allow the beans to stand at room temperature for 12 hours.

2. Drain and rinse the beans, then transfer them to a large pot. Fill the pot with enough fresh water to cover the beans by a few inches. Add the salt.

3. Set the pot over medium-high heat and bring to a simmer. Once simmering, remove the pot from the heat. Drain the beans and rinse gently.

4. Wipe out the pot and return it to the stove over medium-high heat. Add the bacon and cook until it begins to render fat. Add the onion and carrots. Sauté until the bacon is browned and the vegetables are softened, about 8 to 10 minutes.

5. Add the beans and bay leaves to the pot. Pour in the chicken stock, ensuring the beans are covered by at least 3 inches of liquid.

6. Bring the mixture to a simmer. Continue cooking until the beans are fully softened, about 1½ hours. Keep an eye on the pot and turn down the heat if the mixture begins to boil.

7. Add the vinegar and adjust salt and pepper to taste. Remove the pot from the heat. Discard the bay leaves and any large pieces of carrot and onion.

8. Ladle 1 cup of beans with a bit of liquid from the pot into a blender. Puree on low until fully smooth, increasing the speed if needed.

9. Pour the pureed beans back into the pot and stir to combine. Serve immediately with a side of hot sauce, if desired.

CORNBREAD

1. Preheat the oven to 375°F. Place a 10-inch cast-iron skillet in the oven while it preheats.

2. In a medium bowl, whisk together the cornmeal, flour, baking powder, baking soda, and salt.

3. In a separate bowl, whisk together the eggs, honey, and melted butter until combined.

4. Pour the liquid mixture into the dry mixture and begin to whisk. Add the buttermilk and continue whisking until the ingredients form a thick batter. A few lumps are okay!

5. Remove the hot skillet from the oven and pour the batter into it. Return the skillet to the middle rack of the oven.

6. Bake for 25 to 30 minutes, or until a toothpick inserted in the center comes out clean.

7. Remove the skillet from the oven and allow to cool for at least 30 minutes before serving.

The Tropical Trish

DIFFICULTY

MAKES 1 DRINK
PREP TIME: 5 MINUTES

This is definitely some of the good stuff. This refreshing *Barb and Star*–inspired cocktail will make you feel like you've been whisked away to a sunny beach even if it's the middle of winter! You'll want to serve this in a tall, chilled glass. I like to add a little pineapple wedge cut in the shape of a star as the perfect garnish! Triple the recipe and you'll have enough to fill a punchbowl. Bonus points if you can make a pirate ship out of papaya to go on top like in the movie!

1½ ounces Reba's Place Pineapple-Infused Rum (p. 197)

1 ounce blue Curaçao

2 ounces pineapple juice

1 ounce creme de coconut

½ ounce mango juice

½ ounce fresh lemon juice

½ cup ice, plus more as needed

Pineapple wedge or orange slice, for garnish

1. Place rum, Curaçao, juices, creme de coconut, and ice in a high-powered blender and blend until slushy.

2. Pour into a tall, chilled cocktail glass. Garnish with a pineapple wedge or orange slice and enjoy!

The Fancy

DIFFICULTY

2 ounces whiskey
(I love Blanton's)

Squeeze of lime juice

6 ounces 7UP or Sprite

Lime wedge, for garnish

I like a lot of different drinks, but I always come back to my old standby—my version of a seven and seven. I've adapted it over the years as my tastes have changed. It's the closest thing I have to a signature drink—The Fancy.

1. Fill a highball glass with ice. Add the whiskey, lime juice, and soda. Stir gently to mix.

2. Garnish with a lime wedge and enjoy!

Like It Not That Fancy?

If you'd like a non-alcoholic version, swap the whiskey for cranberry juice.

Acknowledgments

Every band is only as good as the members in it, and I've found that making a book is pretty much like that too. To my siblings, Alice, Susie, and Pake, you're the best friends I could ever ask for, and I'm so grateful for the fun memories our family shares. I wouldn't be the person I am today without y'all, and I look up to each of you in different ways. To Shelby, who gave me the blessed gift of being a mom. To my good friend Garth Brooks, who generously lent his voice to the foreword of this book. You make all of us Okies so proud. To the rest of my family, friends, bandmates, and coworkers—from Oklahoma to Tennessee to New York to California— you inspired so many of these stories, and I'm so lucky to have crossed paths with so many fun and brilliant people through the years. And to all my fans who have taken each journey with me with excitement and encouragement—y'all are the best!

I'm so grateful to my team over at Harper Celebrate, led by my publisher, Michael Aulisio, whose vision and constant commitment made this project possible. I'm also thankful to my editor, Danielle Peterson, for your collaboration throughout the creative development; to my creative director, Sabryna Lugge, for capturing my style on every page; to designer Emily Ghattas for making these interiors shine; to my editorial director Marilyn Jansen, for corralling the moving parts; and to Jennifer Gott for ensuring every detail is just right. And of course, to my marketing lead Robin Richardson for originating so many creative ideas; and to publicity director MacKenzie Collier and marketer Mandy Wilson for ensuring that this book finds the hands of our readers.

Thank you to my right-hand man, Justin McIntosh, who I can count on for just about anything. You're one of the best in the business. So much of this book was made possible because of you. Thank you to my brand manager, wardrobe stylist, and go-to for anything and everything, Leslie Matthews. To my tour manager, Marne McLyman, who has kept me on track and where I needed to be, thank you for your hard work through these many years. And my hair and makeup stylist, Neil Robison. It's always comforting to know y'all are there helping me look my best and be on time where I need to be. Y'all sure do keep me laughing!

To my collaborator, Molly Hodgin, thank you for helping me bring my stories to the page. To my photographer, Robby Klein, you're a genius at what you do, and you always know how to capture the spirit of the moment. Thanks to your team: digital technician Andres Martinez, and assistants David Johnson, Allysa Barker, and Garrett French for their work making our photoshoot so fun and easy. To producer Kris D'Amico, photographer Nick Bumgardner, food stylist and recipe tester Sara Mellas, and lighting technician Daniel Williams, many thanks for your collective work to make the food photography look absolutely mouthwatering.

To the talented Chef Kurtess Mortensen and the Choctaw Nation, I'm so grateful for your partnership on our restaurant and for your generous contributions to the book. And to all my friends and family who contributed recipes—Lucchese Luchsinger, Susie McEntire, Chris Rich, Lise Davis, Nikki Spalaris, Katy McEntire, Shane Tarleton, Kix Brooks, Lori Turner, Carolyn Berry, Terry Gordon—y'all are just so generous and talented, and we're eating well because of you.

And to Rex Linn, for being the funniest man I know. You're a dork, Sugar Tot, and you make everything a little bit sweeter. Love you!

And mostly, to my mama and daddy looking down on us, thank you for never letting us forget where we came from and what really matters most in life.

Recipe Index

Scan here for Reba's albums, including her new release, *Not That Fancy*, which features thirteen stripped-down acoustic versions of her iconic hits, plus the brand-new song "Seven Minutes in Heaven."

Available now on vinyl, CD, and your favorite streaming platform.

About the Author

Multimedia entertainment mogul Reba McEntire has become a household name through a successful career that includes music, television, film, theater, retail, and hospitality. The Country Music Hall of Fame and Hollywood Bowl member has more than 50 award wins under her belt, earning honors from the Academy of Country Music (ACM) Awards, American Music Awards, People's Choice Awards, Country Music Association (CMA) Awards, GRAMMY® Awards, and Gospel Music Association (GMA) Dove Awards. Reba was also a 2018 Kennedy Center Honors recipient in addition to multiple philanthropic and leadership honors.

Reba has celebrated unprecedented success, including 35 career number one singles and more than 58 million albums sold worldwide. Reba earned her 60th Top 10 on the Billboard Country Airplay chart, extending her record for the most Top 10 hits among female artists. Reba's Top 10 success spans five straight decades, landing her in the singular group with only George Jones, Willie Nelson, and Dolly Parton, who have the same achievement.

The Oklahoma native and Golden Globe®–nominated actress has multiple movie credits to her name, a critically acclaimed lead role on Broadway in Irving Berlin's *Annie Get Your Gun*, and starred in the six-season television sitcom *Reba*. Reba has also proven to be a savvy entrepreneur, with longstanding brand partnerships that include her Dillard's clothing line and her western footwear collection REBA by Justin™. She has even added restaurateur to the list with Reba's Place, a restaurant, bar, retail, and entertainment venue in Atoka, Oklahoma. For more information, visit www.Reba.com.